The LINCOLNSHIRE *Cook Book*

A celebration of the amazing food & drink on our doorstep.
Featuring over 35 stunning recipes.

The Lincolnshire Cook Book

©2015 Meze Publishing. All rights reserved.

First edition printed in 2015 in the UK.

ISBN: 978-1-910863-05-3

Compiled by: Lisa Pullen

Written by: Nicola Hall

Thank you to Colin and Bex McGurran, Rachel Green

Photography by: Marc Barker, Tim Green and Sam Bowles
www.marcabarker.com

www.timgreenphotographer.co.uk

www.portraitcollective.com

Edited by: Rachel Heward

Designed by: Paul Cocker, Phil Turner, Marc Barker

Cover art: Luke Prest, www.lukeprest.com

Contributors: Kelsie Marsden, Faye Bailey, Kerre Chen

Published by Meze Publishing Limited

Unit 1 Beehive Works

Milton Street

Sheffield S3 7WL

web: www.mezepublishing.co.uk

Tel: 0114 275 7709

email: info@mezepublishing.co.uk

FOREWORD

"All of our chefs are in the fields just as much as they're in the kitchen, and our menus have benefited all the more for it. We're able to experiment with what's in season and ensure our livestock is looked after to the highest standard."
Colin McGurran - Winteringham Fields

I fell in love with Winteringham Fields and moved to Lincolnshire and it wasn't long before the county itself had claimed me. From the amazing flats of the Wolds, seal spotting at Donna Nook, sailing on the mighty Humber, getting to know local farmers and game managers, to sitting on the back of my Landy having a sundowner with the family whilst watching the children chase the dogs about. This beautiful and diverse county has become home, I never thought I would cease to yearn for the desert plains of the United Arab Emirates. I never thought I would take umbrage to someone being remotely disparaging about the Humber River being dirty, but I can wax lyrical about what a great water it is to anyone's satisfaction. Although I will need a few generations under my belt to be a true local, I love my little corner of this great county.

Before coming here, I would source all of my produce from the best possible suppliers – wherever they were. However as I got more into the rhythm of Winteringham Fields I soon realised most of what I needed was available right on my doorstep. We're an agricultural region, meaning we're home to some fantastic crops of cabbages, cauliflowers and barley, not to mention high welfare farms keeping free-range cattle, pigs and chickens. We have our fair share of game too; pheasant, partridge and venison are bountiful when in season.

As we delved into our own livestock, keeping chickens and sheep, we met a village farmer willing to let us use his great knowledge and land to the restaurant's benefit, Alan Smith grows whatever cabbage I can dream up. This decision has transformed our lives and opened my eyes to a better, healthier and more wholesome way of living. All of our chefs are in the fields each morning before the kitchen, muddy boots lined up by the back door, and our menus have benefited all the more for it. We're able to experiment with what's in season and ensure our livestock is looked after to the highest standard.

It's an inspiring place to live and work and it was here that I came up with my winning 'Quail In The Woods' dish for The Great British Menu. The countryside of Lincolnshire evokes such vivid sights, sounds and smells; one autumnal morning the mist in the trees slowly sinking to the damp woodland floor and a shrill call of quail in the distance was spectacular to behold, and it struck me I could recreate these senses in a dish made from entirely local produce.

I am more creative in the kitchen because of this special place, and judging from the rest of the dishes in this book, so too are the other chefs, foodies and people of this county. We invite you to make the most out of it yourselves. Bon appetit!

Colin McGurran

CONTENTS

Welcome to LINCOLNSHIRE

Lincolnshire's endless green fields have long been fruitful farming pastures which have provided Britain with some of the finest quality produce. Today it stands firmly within the centre of a foodie revolution with hard-working farming communities, a blossoming restaurant scene and local food producers harnessing everything that the rich Lincolnshire soil has to offer.

When it comes to natural beauty, the idyllic setting of the Lincolnshire Wolds and the sandy beaches of the coastline provide the dramatic backdrop to Lincolnshire's flourishing food scene. Much of the sprawling countryside is dominated by the large farming communities which have shaped Lincolnshire's landscape, culture and economy over the decades and Lincolnshire does well to preserve its spectacular scenery whilst harvesting quality yields every summer.

The nutrient rich soils have provided barley and sugar beet with fantastic crop growths year upon year of potatoes, cabbages, onions and more. The iconic Lincolnshire sausages, haslets and stuffed chine are still being hand-crafted using methods and recipes that have been passed down through generations of farmers and butchers. The Select Lincolnshire Sausage Festival annually celebrates their most popular dish allowing chefs and avid cooks to get creative with a variety of flavours, also hosting demonstrations to continue with the old-fashioned techniques.

Many farms still breed and butcher their own meats which include Lincolnshire's premium free-range pork, beef and lamb; packed with authentic flavour and sold in shops and restaurants both within the county and beyond. Many restaurants also head to Grimsby docks for exquisite fresh fish and seafood produce caught in the North Sea; whether it be for a Mediterranean influenced seafood pasta or a good-old fashioned serving of fish and chips.

Lincolnshire's classic plum bread is also not to be missed alongside their artisan baked breads, signature cheeses, chutneys and jams created with the countryside's summer fruits – all delivered far and wide with roots that lead back to this wonderfully resourceful county.

Keeping things local is very important to the people of Lincolnshire which is why their farm shops, markets, delis, restaurants and cafés work hard to help create the heart and soul of this thriving food culture. From Louth to Grantham, Skegness to Boston; you will find a number of foodie havens – many of which are award-winning establishments ran by the most passionate chefs and waiting staff around.

In this book you will find many of these brilliant eateries, businesses and producers who have each dedicated their careers to showcasing and celebrating the excellent produce for which Lincolnshire is known. Fantastically unique in every way possible, Lincolnshire leads the way with a healthy dose of nostalgia when it comes to food.

Here you will discover some inspirational recipes to get you experimenting in the kitchen. Whether you're a local hoping to recreate beloved family favourites or a cooking novice who loves to try out new things; Lincolnshire is a promising dining destination that continues to keep the spirit of tradition alive through food.

We Only Select the Best of LINCOLNSHIRE

Showcasing the greatest Lincolnshire produce to celebrate the county's food, drink, flowers and farming industry the Select Lincolnshire brand has become the collective voice of Lincolnshire's finest businesses.

Showcasing the greatest Lincolnshire produce to celebrate the county's food, drink, flower and farming industry, the Select Lincolnshire brand has become the collective voice of Lincolnshire's finest businesses.

Working with some of Lincolnshire's most treasured restaurants, hotels, farm shops and food businesses, Select Lincolnshire set out to show the rest of the UK that Lincolnshire is the jewel in the British food industry's crown, thanks to its rich history of traditional farming methods and skills that have been handed down through generations.

Lincolnshire has a very distinguished agricultural and horticultural heritage, exporting some of the finest produce in the UK year after year. The diversity of ingredients available within the county's boundaries inspires unique and innovative dishes throughout the region. Select Lincolnshire work to promote this rich industry to the steadily rising number of tourists visiting the county each year.

With a wealth of award-winning butchers and farm shops selling everything from free-range pork, stuffed chine and Lincolnshire sausages, as well as locally bred beef and free-range lamb, it's no wonder the rest of the country often looks to the region for the highest quality meat on offer.

And it doesn't stop there, other businesses in Select Lincolnshire's portfolio include those producing and dealing in organic vegetables, handmade cheeses, baked goods and more, trading not just locally but nationwide too.

Annually hosting the Food, Drink and Hospitality Awards, Select Lincolnshire gives credit where credit is due to the hard working individuals who make this county an exciting and thriving place for diners. Another event to watch out for in the culinary calendar is The Lincolnshire Food and Gift Fair, kicking off the festive season each year, offering a snapshot of the vibrant and colourful hand-crafted foods and gifts made by the community.

With a membership that grows year upon year, Select Lincolnshire creates a lasting reputation for the county, showing Britain and beyond just what a truly special place it is to be.

We're a county full of food experts. Growers, producers, processors and artisan businesses collectively make up a huge thriving community; from the Humber to the Wash, traditional skills of farming and food production have been nurtured and handed down through the generations to create a rich and diverse food heritage.

Farming is big business for Lincolnshire. Worth around £1 billion to the county's economy, the range of produce is mouth-watering; from cereals and cauliflowers, fudge and handmade ice-cream to marbled Lincoln red beef and Lincolnshire sausages. There's no doubt that the latter are one of the county's most famous exports, with their distinctive peppery taste. Nowhere in the world makes them tastier than our very own county butchers, many of whom use recipes that have been around for decades.

Boston Stump

Belton House

Caistor

The Red Arrows

Fair at Lincoln Cathedral

Exchequer Gate

PiNK PiG FARM
FREERANGE HOMEMADE HAPPINESS

d Enderby smoking haddock

Modens
Gold Award Winning
Lincolnshire
Plum Bread
400g
1936 Recipe

Modens

Modens
Gold Award Winning
Lincolnshire
Plum Bread
400g
1936 Recipe

Jack Bucks Daffodils

Mountains Boston Sausage

Cote Hill Cheese

Lincolnshire Sausage Festival

Lincolnshire Red Cattle

And who could resist cutting a slice of Lincolnshire pork pie with flaky pastry and succulent meat from one of our many award-winning producers? Other Lincolnshire specialties include jams, chutneys, dressings and marmalades that can be found for sale in nearly all local farm shops; and you'll find many artisan bakers and cheese makers selling to their customers at one of the numerous farmers' markets around Lincolnshire and beyond.

But if you'd rather be cooked for, you'll be spoilt for choice with countless pubs, restaurants, hotels and tearooms expertly making the most of Lincolnshire sourced ingredients with innovative and tempting dishes.

Our family

Select Lincolnshire has developed over ten years, and today their members are supported in growing their business through networking, training and one-to-one development opportunities.

With members passionate about their produce, customers and visitors (whether local or travelled) are encouraged to enjoy the best experience, meaning they come back time and again. Thousands of consumers follow Select Lincolnshire, with regular news and updates sent out via print, web and social media.

Select Lincolnshire members are often family businesses with generations of history to their name. Naturally, there is a great sense of community across the whole county; the second largest in the country, it's no wonder it's often referred to as the breadbasket of Britain. Select Lincolnshire is a family too, and members look out for each other by spreading the word far and wide about the quality of their neighbour's products. Everyday Select Lincolnshire encourages members to work together to create new products, tap into new markets and delight even more customers.

Creative, talented and unique

Select Lincolnshire is supported by Lincolnshire Chamber of Commerce and Industry. Their members benefit from wider business support including export advice and avenues to business savings, industry experts, sector forums and a lobbying support network. Through the Lincolnshire Chamber of Commerce, Select Lincolnshire members get direct access to core business support. Events around funding opportunities, training seminars and award ceremonies - not to mention PR and media support - all form part of the package on offer. What sets Select Lincolnshire apart from other organisations is the 360 degree business support available, and the wealth of expert mentors and advisors on call.

Whilst the Lincolnshire sausage may be seen as one of the greatest exports of the county, Select Lincolnshire is uniquely positioned to help all members sell their edible delights across the globe. The Lincolnshire Chamber's exporting team is on hand to identify new overseas markets for local producers, as well as invite them on trade missions and give them a helping hand with the paperwork.

It's simple; there is no other body that supports businesses over the whole of the region. Armed with a wealth of knowledge and expertise, Select Lincolnshire not only assist food and drink businesses, but also support all sectors whether it is engineering, information technology, customer service, tourism or leisure.

They build bespoke support for even the smallest of members working out of their own kitchen, right through to sitting down around board tables of multi-national companies. Being able to offer such a wide range of advice and support makes Select Lincolnshire a truly unique project.

Annual highlights

Lincolnshire has a wealth of local farmers' markets taking place across the whole of the county. From car parks to corn hills, highstreets and village halls – there's always something planned. But if you are looking for something more special, there are some real treats hosted throughout the year to look out for.

During the annual Discover Lincolnshire Weekend in March, the region's producers gather together to help visitors discover the culinary delights on offer locally. Over the summer an action packed calendar of events, from Skegness to Stamford, Gainsborough and Lincoln city see myriad food stalls and markets pop up. The ever popular Lincolnshire Show also takes place each year in June, and sees visitors enjoying the traditions of a proper country show alongside fun family entertainment and the ever-popular shop lined mews.

In the autumn the Lincoln Sausage Festival attracts thousands of people celebrating the famous sage infused delicacy. If you are feeling festive around November and truly love Christmas shopping, thousands of visitors come along to the Lincolnshire Christmas Food and Gift Fair, at the Lincolnshire Showground. It's bursting with local producers all under one roof; you'll be truly surprised at what Lincolnshire can offer you.

As well as these, Select Lincolnshire also represents Lincolnshire at huge trade shows such as the International Food Exhibition, and contacts made at such events have resulted in more Lincolnshire collaborations and delicious food and drink appearing in supermarkets and high-end delis across the UK.

Fun facts

Oslinc, a family run ostrich farming business, sells ostrich eggs at its farmers' markets and recommends you boil them in a jam pan for 40 minutes to get the biggest dippy egg you've ever seen!

We have at least seven bakeries in Lincolnshire making the famous Lincolnshire plum bread, which tastes wonderful if served with a slice of Lincolnshire poacher cheese.

There are at least 80 micro-breweries in Lincolnshire, and Wainfleet near Skegness is home to the famous award-winning Batemans Brewery.

Uncle Henry's won the best sausage award on BBC's The One Show.

Woolsthorpe Manor in Lincolnshire was home to Sir Isaac Newton, and the apple tree can still be seen in the garden!

Lincoln Castle is home to one of only four surviving copies of the Magna Carta.

George Boole, the man who discovered computer logic came from Lincolnshire.

There are a handful of vineyards in Lincolnshire, and from the little Lincolnshire Wolds town called Somersby you can currently buy a bottle of their Magna Carta wine. It is also stocked in Waitrose (November 2015).

With Lincolnshire holding the largest volume of grade one soil in the country – the best in the UK, it's no wonder that it is the largest producer of potatoes, wheat, poultry and cereal.

Lincolnshire produces around 20% of all UK Food with 60% of Britain's cauliflowers growing in Lincolnshire.

Lincolnshire is the UK's largest producer of potatoes, wheat, poultry and cereal.

Lincolnshire is the second largest sugar beet producer in the UK.

Lincolnshire is the fifth largest pork producer in England.

Lincolnshire is the UK's pumpkin capital. The fertile flatlands of the Lincolnshire Fens are not only the traditional centre of the nation's flower bulb industry, but they also produce most of the Halloween pumpkins sold across the nation. Each October Spalding stages it very own pumpkin festival to celebrate, including a pumpkin lantern-lit parade led by… a pumpkin coach, of course.

What links worldwide TV smash hits Call the Midwife and Downton Abbey with a Victorian time capsule? The answer is Lincoln Castle's beautifully preserved Victorian prison. For Call the Midwife, the atmospheric building portrayed a 1950s London women's prison; while for Downton, it stood in for York Prison, where valet John Bates, played by Brendan Coyle, served time.

More information:
www.selectlincolnshire.com
Facebook /LoveFoodSelectLincolnshire
Twitter @LoveFoodLincs
select@lincs-chamber.co.uk

Winteringham Fields

Pumpkin Pasta

Cook grated pumpkin
flesh in olive oil for
15 mins (until it breaks
apart). Add tomato puree,
sour cream or creme fraiche,
½ tsp chilli powder &
cook 'til heated through
pour sauce over cooked
pasta, mix well, eat

Pumpkins
Large £4 each
medium £2.50 each
squash £2.40kg

Doddington Hall   *Elms Farm Cottages*

klington's Bakery

Slice of NOSTALGIA

Bunty's Tearoom is the perfect mixture of
vintage values and good old-fashioned baking.

There's something quite chic and nostalgic about sipping English tea with a delicious slice of cake, no one serves up a better cuppa than Bunty's Tea Room in Lincolnshire. A vintage inspired traditional tea room which opened in 2012; Bunty's Tea Room is the brainchild of Jen Lock, who formerly worked for a sponsorship and promotions company and Matt Felgate, who served in the RAF.

Owing their idea to Jen's grandma Barbara, the pair combined Matt's love of all things vintage and Jen's passion for baking to create the warm and cosy atmosphere of their tea shop, aptly named after good old 'Granny Bunty'.

Located in a cosy, old-fashioned Grade II listed building halfway up Lincolnshire's award-winning street Steep Hill, this retro inspired tea shop is heaven for lovers of vintage country style.

Serving up scones with clotted cream and jam, sandwiches, handmade cakes and their famous afternoon tea, Bunty's Tea Room freshly prepares all of their food with locally-sourced ingredients alongside delicious brews in a variety of both classic and fruity flavours.

What truly sets Bunty's apart from the rest is their selection of homemade cakes, using combinations of unusual flavours for a delicious taste experience that would make Mary Berry proud. Jen regularly experiments with exciting new concoctions for her signature bakes, using non-traditional ingredients such as Pimm's, dandelion and burdock and even Marmite.

Bunty's have the tiniest details perfected, serving everything on mismatched China tea cups and fine bone China plates. Kitsch décor and 1950s posters adorn the walls, big band music plays in the background, fresh cut flowers sit on each table and family photos give a personal and familiar touch which welcomes guests with a smile. Bunty's even host events in their quaint little shop, catering for birthday parties and baby showers with a sugary dose of sweet and sentimental style.

Since their opening, Jen and Matt have earned a top rating on Trip Advisor and have won at The National Vintage Awards for their vintage inspired events; something which reflects the hard work they've put in to making Bunty's much more than your regular café or lunchtime spot. However, the real proof is in the pudding as their afternoon tea and lunch menu regularly sees customers queuing out of the door to what has become one of Lincolnshire's most fun and welcoming venues.

Bunty's Tea Room
PIMM'S CAKE

A delicious cake made using the classic summer drink Pimm's
topped with fresh cucumber, strawberries and mint.

Ingredients

For the cake:

450g caster sugar

450g self-raising flour

450g softened butter

2 tsp baking powder

8 large eggs

8 large strawberries, chopped

16 fresh mint leaves, chopped

3 tbsp Pimm's

For the buttercream:

250g softened butter

500g icing sugar

3 tbsp Pimm's

For decoration:

8 large strawberries

10 fresh mint leaves

½ cucumber, sliced with peeler

3 tbsp strawberry jam

Method

For the cake

Heat your oven to 180°C.

Lightly grease and line two 10" cake tins.

Cream the butter and sugar together until light in texture and colour.

Scrape down the sides of the bowl.

Add the flour, eggs, baking powder and Pimm's and mix until thoroughly combined.

Fold in the mint and strawberries.

Transfer the mixture to sandwich tins and bake for 30 minutes.

For the buttercream

Mix icing sugar, butter and Pimm's until pale.

Once the cake has completely cooled spoon the jam onto the top of one sponge.

Spread the buttercream onto the bottom of the second sponge and carefully place one on top of the other.

Spread the remaining buttercream on top of the cake (with optional piping).

Decorate with cucumber, mint leaves and strawberries.

Destination Dining at
DODDINGTON

With its walled kitchen garden and estate supplying the freshest zero food miles ingredients, Doddington is the perfect destination to indulge your passion for top quality, seasonal, local, delicious food – either dining in or taking away ingredients to release your inner Nigella (or Jamie) at home!

Doddington is without question, a captivating dining destination. Standing in the middle of a small village just outside of Lincoln, its farm shop, café and restaurant are at the centre of an inspiring re-invention of the traditional country estate for the 21st Century. The Hall's sprawling gardens are filled with colour all year round, its mellow Elizabethan brickwork is beautiful, its history is fascinating and its interior is filled with original artwork and furniture. Perhaps most surprising of all is that Doddington Hall has endured over 400 years of unbroken family occupation.

Built by Robert Smythson, registrar to the Bishop of Lincoln in 1595, the Hall has been passed down through the Hussey, Delaval and Jarvis families until Claire Birch (nee Jarvis) and her husband James took on the Hall from Claire's parents in 2006. They are both extremely passionate and utterly devoted to this stunning and unique building, and the surrounding estate which has become a central historic attraction of Lincolnshire.

Claire and James decided to leave their own mark on Doddington by restoring the walled kitchen garden and opening a farm shop, café and restaurant in 2007 to showcase the wonderful produce grown there. Here you can find also beef, game, honey and foraged wild food from the estate alongside other locally-sourced produce.

Doddington reared Lincoln Red beef is a favourite on the restaurant menu with a medley of locally-reared free-range meats available to purchase from their butchery counter. The deli hosts local artisan cheeses and British charcuterie, the bakery stocks bread baked in a wood-fired ovens from nearby bakeries whilst biscuits, cakes and pastries are baked daily on the premises alongside larder essentials such as jams, chutneys and sauces made from the ripe and delicious fruit and veg grown in their very own soil.

The Doddington restaurant and café provides charming views of restored farm buildings and the surrounding parkland. The creative use of home-grown Lincolnshire produce put together by the hardworking chefs at Doddington has seen Doddington café and restaurant shortlisted for the 2015 Great Food Club Awards, a gold listing from Lincolnshire Life's Taste Awards as well as winning the FARMA 'Farm Restaurant and Café Of The Year' in 2015.

Claire and James have certainly revived Doddington for a new generation, introducing visitors from near and far to their wonderful historical estate and inspiring English food. Whether stopping by for afternoon tea or booking for a very special wedding, Doddington Hall has re-written its own history to become one of the must-see attractions of Lincolnshire for explorers and foodies alike.

Pistachio & Honey Cake

Doddington Hall
RABBIT SCOTCH EGG

with picked carrot, chard purée and black pudding soil.

Serves 4.

Ingredients

For the Scotch egg:

4 large free-range eggs

200g Lincolnshire sausage meat

200g minced rabbit and/or other game such as partridge, pheasant or pigeon.

Salt and freshly ground black pepper

125g plain flour, seasoned with salt and freshly ground black pepper

4 free-range eggs, beaten

400g breadcrumbs

Vegetable oil, for deep frying

For the black pudding soil:

150g black pudding, cooked

For the pickled carrot:

6 baby carrots

400ml water

200ml olive oil

200ml white wine vinegar

100g sugar

2 sprigs thyme

For the chard purée:

Handful of washed chard

20g butter

50ml cream

Method

Place the eggs, still in their shells, in a pan of boiling salted water and simmer for 6 minutes. Drain and cool the eggs under cold running water, then peel.

Mix the rabbit mince with the sausage in a bowl and season well with salt and freshly ground black pepper. Divide the mixture into four and flatten each section out on a 40cm x 40cm squared piece of cling film, shaping into ovals which are about 12.5cm long and 7.5cm wide.

Place each egg onto a sausage and rabbit meat oval, then pick the cling film square up by its corners, using it to wrap the sausage meat around each egg. Make sure the coating is smooth and completely covers the egg.

Roll each one in flour, then in the beaten egg, rolling to coat all over before rolling in the breadcrumbs to completely cover. Repeat this process with each egg.

Put all the pickling liquor ingredients in a saucepan, bring to the boil and simmer for three minutes. Add carrots to the liquor and simmer for two minutes, then remove and set to one side before refrigerating for later.

Bring a pan of water to the boil and blanch the chard for one minute; then refresh in cold water. Heat up the butter and cream on a low heat taking care not to boil, add the chard and cook for two minutes. Use a hand blender and turn into a purée.

Heat the oil in a deep heavy-bottomed pan. Check for the correct temperature by dropping in a breadcrumb to see if it sizzles and turns brown.

Carefully place each scotch egg into the hot oil and deep-fry for 7-8 minutes, until golden and crisp and sausage meat is completely cooked. Carefully remove from the oil with a slotted spoon and drain on kitchen paper.

Break up the pieces of cooked black pudding and scatter on a plate to resemble 'soil' and place the scotch egg on top of the chard purée with the pickled carrots on top of the soil to garnish.

Doddington Hall
MULBERRY FRANGIPANE

Being completely gluten-free, this cake is good for you as well as delicious.
Serves 8.

Ingredients

250g butter

250g caster sugar

6 whole eggs

250g ground almonds

250g ground rice

100g mulberries or any other
seasonal fruit such as plums,
rhubarb, raspberries, strawberries,
blackberries, figs, apples or cherries

To serve:

Chopped almonds

Powdered sugar

Vanilla ice cream

Fresh fruit

Method

Pre-heat the oven to 150°C.

Cream together butter and sugar in a mixer until light and fluffy.

Add the eggs one at a time keeping the mixer on until incorporated fully.

Add all the dry ingredients to the mix.

Pour into an 8" cake tin and top with the mulberries or a seasonal fruit of your choice.

Bake at 150°C for approximately 1 hour until golden.

To serve, sprinkle on a few chopped almonds and some powdered sugar. Add vanilla ice cream and more fresh fruit if you like.

Chip Off The OLD BLOCK

Lincolnshire is fortunate to be home to the Tweedale family, and in Elite, one of the best fish and chip shops in the country.

There's nothing quite like traditional British fish and chips and whilst each county has its own unique traditions and tastes, Lincolnshire is lucky to have one of the country's finest.

Opened in 1988, this business has family roots which go back three generations to David Tweedale and his wife Freda who started up their first fish shop in Huddersfield in 1972. Sourcing fresh fish from the docks of Hull, their son Adrian soon became a 'chip off the old block' and at 15 began working towards building his very own fish and chip takeaway using locally-sourced ingredients and a strong hard-working spirit.

The Elite branch in the sleepy Ruskington Village was opened sixteen years later, and still upholds the important values of great quality food and excellent customer service that David and Freda worked hard to achieve. In David's own words. 'If it isn't broke, don't fix it'.

Today, Adrian owns a second shop in Lincoln which seats up to 100 people. His daughter Rachel, who is Elite's third-generation fryer also opened up a third restaurant in Sleaford in 2012 and was named the 2015 Drywite Young Fish Fryer of the Year.

Rachel is keen to carry on her family's reputation among the locals who are always welcomed with open arms, ensuring that Elite is a place people will always return to with their friends and family for many years to come.

Working to ethically source all of their ingredients with as few food miles as possible, they still import their sustainable, high quality fish from the Hull and Grimsby docks whilst the potatoes for their award-winning chips are grown right on their doorstep. All of their seafood products are MSC certified meaning that they can trace their cod, haddock and prawns to ensure that the fish has been caught responsibly and ethically.

Meanwhile, their salads and garnishes are made with the produce from local farmers markets whilst the classic fish and chip batter recipe is the same one that has been used in the family for over 40 years.

It's clearly working. Back in 1992 they were named National Fish and Chip Shop of the Year; it's this standard that the Tweedale family aspire to each day. However it is their customer loyalty that is the real winner for Elite as the staff and guests are truly made to feel part of the family.

Elite's
FISH PLATTER

We recommend using sustainably sourced British fish to create this smorgasboard of seafood classics. Serves 4.

Ingredients

200g cod fillet

200g haddock fillet

8 langoustine tails (shelled and de-veined)

800g Maris Piper potatoes

Beef dripping for frying

200g marrowfat peas

2 tsp bicarbonate of soda

Salt

400g plain flour

2 tsp baking powder

Cold water

For the tartare sauce:

250ml good quality mayonnaise

3 tbsp capers

3 tbsp gherkins

1 shallot

3 tbsp parsley

Squeeze of lemon

Method

Pour the marrowfat peas in water in a deep saucepan and allow to steep overnight, allowing them to double in size. Ensure that there is enough water to accommodate this.

Drain the peas and pour over fresh water whilst adding two teaspoons of bicarbonate of soda and one teaspoon of salt. Bring to the boil and then allow peas to simmer, stirring often until they turn soft and mushy.

Measure out 600ml of cold water into a bowl and place in the fridge to chill ready for making the batter. The colder the water, the crispier the batter so aim for a temperature of about 5°C.

Once the water is cold enough add two teaspoons of baking powder and two teaspoons of salt.

Slowly add the flour to the water, whisking continuously until you have a smooth batter with the consistency of single cream.

Place the batter back in to the fridge for at least 30 minutes to chill again.

Peel your potatoes and cut in to thick chips. The thicker the chip, the less dripping they will absorb when fried.

Portion the cod and haddock into four 50g portions.

Slowly heat the beef dripping to 190°C.

Whilst waiting for the dripping to heat, finely chop the capers, shallot, gherkins and parsley before mixing in to the mayonnaise.

Add a squeeze of lemon and place the tartare sauce in the fridge to chill.

Once the dripping is at the correct temperature, place the chips into the fryer and allow to cook for 5-6 minutes. Chips should be crispy on the outside and fluffy on the inside once cooked.

To cook the fish, place it in the batter ensuring it is covered evenly and lay each piece into the dripping.

Allow to cook for approximately 4-5 minutes, turning the fish to cook on both sides until the batter is golden and crispy. Note that the langoustines may cook quicker than the cod and haddock.

Allow the fish to drain before plating up alongside the chips, mushy peas and a good dollop of tartare sauce!

Keeping it in
THE FAMILY

Versatile with savoury or sweet dishes, the wartime classic fruit vinegars are making a comeback and at the minute, no one makes them better than Fred and Bex.

Ann and Mark Gedney were always fond of the classic family recipe for raspberry vinegar which had been passed down from generation to generation in the Gedney household. When their children Freddie and Rebecca left home in 2013, they came up with the marvellous idea to develop and bottle their own secret potion and sell it, naming their newfound company after their beloved son and daughter.

Made using all natural ingredients and whole fruits in their Lincolnshire home, their old fashioned handmade fruit vinegars have gained an almost cult following with word spreading far and wide. In fact, Fred and Bex's raspberry and blackberry fruit vinegars won them a total of three gold stars at Great Taste Awards in 2015, introducing the recipes that grandma used to make to a whole new audience.

Today's generations may seldom remember the sharp and sweet taste of a good British fruit vinegar, but the full-flavoured raspberry or blackberry vinegars like those produced by Fred and Bex were integral parts of the post-war pantry. Ann recalls the old lady who recently told her she would have a medicinal spoonful a day, which for Ann, is part of the joy as she loves nothing more than to meet people who love her product, whether it be through nostalgia or a new discovery.

Perfect for an ingredient in fruity pies or stock gravy, chefs such as Rachel Green have been kick-starting a revival of cooking with the classic wartime fruit vinegars and Fred and Bex' are certainly some of the best. Ann developed her great grandmother-in-law's traditional version to give this versatile cooking favourite a new Lincolnshire lease of life not seen since the release of Mrs Beeton's first cookery book back in the Victorian era. Fred and Bex are now well on their way to introducing a whole new age of chefs, foodies and amateur cooks to the wonders of the delicious, tangy fruit flavours.

Designing their own packaging and sourcing their fresh fruit from Lincolnshire as much as possible, Fred and Bex's vinegars are surprisingly adaptable for the modern kitchen. Submitting recipes to their blog on a weekly basis, Ann concocts everything from salad dressings, syrups and cake icing, to adding great swigs to casseroles and tagines, giving your favourite dishes an old fashioned kick with a natural, rich taste.

Fred & Bex
YORKSHIRE PUDDING

with caramelised apples

Serve with Fred and Bex raspberry vinegar or blackberry vinegar if you like.
Serves 4-6.

Ingredients

For the Yorkshire pudding:

100g plain flour

Pinch of salt

3 eggs

225ml milk

2 tbsp sunflower oil

For the caramelised apples:

25g butter

100g caster sugar

500g apples, peeled & cored, cut into thick slices. Cox's or Bramley's are good.

Fred & Bex raspberry or blackberry vinegar to finish

Method

Pre-heat the oven to 240°C.

First make the Yorkshire Pudding

Put flour and salt in a bowl. Make a well in centre of the flour and add the eggs with a little milk.

Whisk to make a smooth paste then add the remaining liquid to make a batter. Set aside.

Next for the caramelised apples

Heat the butter and sugar in a frying pan, let it melt a little, then throw in the apples and cook over a high heat for 3-4 minutes until the apples slightly caramelise and start to soften.

Put the sunflower oil in a suitable roasting tin, and pop into the hot oven.

When the oil is good and hot, throw in the sliced apples and then the Yorkshire pudding batter.

Bake in the oven for 30-40 minutes.

Remove from the oven, liberally dust with icing sugar then slosh on lots of Fred and Bex raspberry or blackberry vinegar. Yum yum!!

Keeping It
LOCAL

It may be new to the Lincolnshire culinary scene, but Harrisons Restaurant in Barton-Upon-Humber is already winning awards for its mix of fine local produce and winning flavour combinations.

As one of Lincolnshire's newest eateries, Harrisons Restaurant is already establishing itself as one of the finest. Situated in the heart of the market place in Barton-Upon-Humber, the name of this award-winning business was inspired by two notable gentleman; John Harrison, the inventor of the first marine chronological clock who lived in the nearby village of Barrow-upon-Humber during the 1700s, and Dandy illustrator Ken Harrison, who is still currently a resident of Barton. Each have had a significant impact on British culture as some of Lincolnshire's proudest exports.

Their name suggests big ambitions, but being a small local restaurant is what Harrisons is all about, chef and owner Peter Storey explains that they are extremely proud to serve and source local produce as part of their menu.

Blessed with the finest fruit and vegetables in the region and some of the best cheese in the UK, Harrisons keep the Lincolnshire spirit alive and well by selecting their smoked fish from Alfred Enderby in Grimsby, their meat from Jason Gray's butchers' and ales from the nearby Tom Wood Brewery to cook and serve it all up with their own unique Harrisons flair.

Whether it be a modern take on an English favourite or interesting twist to the flavours they choose, Harrisons focus on taste and presentation to make any visit a special dining experience.

Day after day, Harrisons serve up their casual bar menu with some delicious beef and pork burgers as well as their restaurant menu and ever-popular Sunday lunches, using rare roast beef as well as other roasted specials such as fish and vegetarian options. Harrisons have managed to hone their culinary skills and excellent service in just over 10 months, winning themselves the Select Lincolnshire Restaurant of the Year award for 2015 and 2016.

With their hard-working team, Harrisons continue to build a base of loyal customers, not just in their native town but beyond. Their collaboration with local artist Jill Smith, whose work appears on the walls at Harrisons, helps to create a comforting and familiar atmosphere to complement their fabulous food which is set to see them snap up many more accolades in the future.

Harrisons Restaurant

Harrisons
SMOKED HADDOCK CHOWDER

Using locally-sourced smoked haddock from Alfred Enderby for an authentic Lincolnshire flavour, this smoked haddock chowder is a warming treat throughout any season. You can buy the fish from www.alfredenderby.co.uk
Serves 4.

Ingredients

500g natural smoked haddock

500g fresh mussels, cleaned

200g pancetta lardons

100g butter

1 leek

4 shallots

600ml milk

100ml cream

30g plain flour

1 tsp Dijon mustard

Pinch salt

Pinch pepper,

Sprig of parsley, chopped

1 bay leaf

White wine

Method

Dice the shallots and wash and slice the leek into 1cm slices.

Put the butter into a heavy based saucepan, soften the shallots and leeks on a medium to low heat for 7-10 minutes.

Clean and de-beard the mussels, discarding any that do not close when tapped.

Turn up to a high heat and add the pancetta lardons, cooking until they start to brown.

Chop the smoked haddock into 2½cm cubes. You can also remove the skin if you prefer.

Cook the haddock in the pan for 3-4 minutes, adding the bay leaf and pepper halfway through.

Add the white wine and leave everything to reduce on a medium heat for around 2-3 minutes.

Tip the flour into the pan and stir in well; this will thicken the mixture.

Add the milk gradually, stirring each time until the mixture thickens further.

Bring the milk to a light boil and add the cream along with the Dijon mustard.

Leave this to simmer on a low heat for 7 minutes.

Add the cleaned mussels to the pan but don't stir through. Turn the heat low and instead put the lid on the pan to steam the mussels open.

Once opened, stir through with the chowder before adding the chopped parsley, salt and pepper to taste and serve.

Harrisons
SEARED VENISON

with Lincolnshire vegetables

This is a simple dish which uses a range of textures and flavours. It relies on good quality ingredients to shine through and Lincolnshire provides all the home-grown essentials to make this dish great. Here at the restaurant we use fallow deer steaks along with locally grown vegetables. Serves 4.

Ingredients

4 x 200g venison steaks

2 shallots, diced

2 sprigs fresh thyme

30ml balsamic vinegar

250ml glass red wine

500ml homemade beef stock

2 large carrots

1 head cauliflower

200g butter

300g sliced kale

Oil, for frying

Salt and pepper, to season

Method

For the red wine reduction, add the diced shallots to a heated saucepan and cook with a splash of oil for 2-4 minutes.

Add fresh thyme leaves with a good splash of balsamic vinegar and cook until this has evaporated. Add a large glass of red wine and reduce to about ⅓ before adding the stock. You can add optional gravy powder if you wish to thicken.

Leave to simmer whilst you prepare the rest of the dish. Peel the carrots taking care to remove the top before cutting into large sections. Place into a pan of water and bring to the boil.

Remove the venison steak from the fridge for 5-10 minutes to take the chill from the meat. Once the water in your pan is boiling, simmer for a further 15 minutes until the carrot feels firm but with a little give when squeezed between the finger and thumb.

Prepare the cauliflower by cutting the florets into small 2½cm pieces.

Place into a saucepan with the butter and sautée until soft.

Boil a pan of water. Whilst the water is heating up, take a cast iron skillet pan or a heavy bottomed frying pan and place on a high heat.

Season the venison with salt and pepper and place into the pan with a splash of oil to prevent sticking. Cook the venison on each side for six minutes for a pink steak or 8-9 minutes each side for a well done finish.

Once the venison is cooked to your liking, remove it from the pan and leave to rest for 3-4 minutes. Place a small piece of butter onto of each steak to help keep it moist whilst it is set aside.

When the venison is resting, put the carrots into a pan with plenty of butter and cook until you achieve an even, brown colour.

When the cauliflower is soft, place into a food processor or blender with the butter and blitz the cauliflower until smooth. Add a pinch of salt to taste if not using salted butter.

Add the sliced kale to the pan of boiling water and cook for 1-2 minutes.

Put a tablespoon of the purée onto the plate and drag it across for presentation.

Place the kale alongside the purée with the carrot before slicing the venison and placing on top the kale. Drizzle the dish with the red wine gravy and serve.

Green, Green Grass
OF HOME

Hidden in the outer echelons of the Lincolnshire Wolds lies The Inn On The Green, one of the county's finest purveyors of top notch pub food.

Sitting on the outer reaches of the Lincolnshire Wolds in the quaint village of Ingham, The Inn On The Green is a hidden gem which honours top quality service, delicious homecooked food and locally-sourced fresh ingredients.

Starting up in March 2005, Sarah Sharpe and Andrew Cafferkey combined their years of experience working in some of London and Essex's finest eateries to open The Inn On The Green situated within a stunning limestone Grade II listed building that stands unpretentiously and welcoming to all. Sarah and Andrew had known each other for 15 years before they decided to start their own business after they met working at Bell Inn and Hill House in Essex. After travelling to Australia, Sarah cut her industry teeth in the Michelin-starred Chapter One restaurant in Bromley whilst Andrew became the head chef at renowned Belgravia dining spot La Poule Au Pot.

They set out to create a business of their own and today, their award-winning restaurant grows its own vegetables, fruit and herbs in a nearby village allotment, some of which is grown by Sarah's father for the freshest and most authentic tasting dishes around.

The Inn On The Green creates new and exciting recipes each day with the help of sous chef Chris Wilburn who focuses on introducing new techniques to make their dishes stand out.

Foraging mushrooms, rosehips, wild garlic and sloes whenever they can to create Andrew's unique homemade chutneys and gin, they have pieced together an ever-changing menu which draws guests from near and far. Sarah, Chris, Andrew and their team try to keep things as local and quintessentially British as possible, counting local businesses like Redhill Farm, Cote Hill Cheese, Horncastle Ales, Simpson's Butchers and Tom Wood Brewery as their suppliers.

The Inn On The Green have over the years worked up quite a reputation amongst visitors and critics alike. They have boasted a main listing in the AA Pub Guide and The Good Pub Guide since 2007, shortly after they opened in 2005, as well as winning the Best Pub Food Restaurant at the Taste Of Excellence Lincolnshire Life Cuisine Awards numerous times. They are also a member of Select Lincolnshire.

A brilliant grazing spot for a fragrant summer lunch looking out into the Lincoln countryside or the perfect destination for an exquisite warming winter meal by the fire, The Inn On The Green is one dining experience you won't want to miss.

The Inn On The Green
PAN-ROASTED CHICKEN BREAST

with sage and onion pudding

This herby chicken dish fuses the best flavours of traditional English cooking for a wholesome, hearty meal. Serves 4.

Ingredients

6 rainbow baby carrots

2 large onions

Four 180g French trim chicken breast, skin on

100g sage

100g thyme

100g suet

100g self-raising flour

100ml chicken stock

100ml cold water

30g sugar

50ml boiling water

Cornflour

Onion crisp for garnish

For red wine jus:

200ml red wine

200ml of beef stock

Method

Dissolve the sugar in boiling water to make a stock syrup.

Slice one of the onions into rings.

Coat the onion rings in the stock syrup and arrange on a non-stick tray so that they resemble the olympic rings. Place in a cool oven at 100°C for 12 hours.

To begin the sage and onion pudding, grate half an onion and add to the flour and suet mix along with 50g of chopped thyme and sage.

Bring the mix together, season and ball to the size of a ten pence piece, equal to approximately 20g.

Poach each pudding ball in boiling salted water for approximately 6 minutes before removing with a spoon and draining. Leave to sit until cold.

For the herb purée, chop the remaining herbs and add to 100ml of boiling chicken stock.

Thicken the stock with a little cornflour and blend to a purée. Season to taste.

Cook your rainbow carrots by adding to boiling water for 5 minutes.

Pan fry the chicken for 2 minutes on each side and then place in the oven skinside down at 185°C for 15 minutes.

In the mean time, warm through your sage and onion puddings in the oven.

On a large plate, place a line of the herb purée in the middle of the plate for presentation.

Cut the now fully cooked chicken in to three triangles and place on top of the purée with warmed pudding balls inbetween each piece of chicken.

Drizzle the red wine jus over the chicken and garnish with the onion crisp and herbs then serve.

House ON THE HILL

One of Lincoln's most iconic buildings on Steep Hill houses one of its most iconic restaurants. And with a former Michelin-starred head chef at the helm, Jews House is going from strength to strength.

Housed in one of the oldest buildings in the city of Lincoln, Jews House is the product of award-winning chef Gavin Aitkenhead and Samantha Tomkins who have been in residence at the restaurant for almost 10 years. Offering exceptional service and food that they themselves love to eat, they cook with the highest quality ingredients, experimenting with new techniques for a menu which stands out from the crowd.

Gavin, a Lincolnshire native, worked his way up to head chef under Germain Schwab from 1998, gaining his experience at the former two Michelin-starred restaurant Winteringham Fields before setting his sights on opening his own restaurant in Lincolnshire.

With the confidence and passion to cook great food, he chose the historic city to be the setting for their business. With Samantha bringing her expertise in hospitality and service, making this dining destination a welcome experience for every guest.

Gavin's philosophy on food has always been simple and solely about originality and flavour. This made him a perfect fit for the prestigious restaurant at Jews House when it became vacant. The Grade I building itself is said to be over 900 years old and located on the notable Steep Hill. It was traditionally associated with the thriving Jewish community in medieval times and today the ornately carved doorway remains. Having been recently restored the building is a fascinating reminder of Lincolnshire's treasured history and is even rumoured to host its own ghosts – just one of the stories surrounding this unique property.

When Jews House re-opened in 2006 with Gavin and Samantha at the helm, the restaurant merged local Lincolnshire produce with culinary influences from across the globe, creating an exquisite a taster menu and varied à la carte menu, showcasing Gavin's skills and expertise in the kitchen.

Whether it be simple food done exceptionally well from their 'Lunch For Less' deal or a special occasion event held in their ancient but inviting little inn, Jews House bring the finest food to the table served by the friendliest staff in a polished, attentive service.

Jews House
ROAST TURBOT, SMOKED MUSSELS,

capers, wild mushrooms and Yukon Gold foam

This twist on a classic fish dish is a real show stopper and easier to prepare
than you may think. Serves 4.

Ingredients

4 x 150g portions turbot, or cod if preferred

600g fresh Scottish mussels, cleaned

100g risotto rice

50g Earl Grey tea leaves

100ml white wine

Bunch of fresh dill

Handful of capers

100g cucumber

200g wild mushrooms

1 tsp grapeseed oil

1 tsp butter

For the potato foam:

200g Yukon Gold potatoes, peeled

100ml potato water

100ml milk

100ml double cream

Pinch of salt and pepper

1 cream whipper, optional

Method

Start by chopping the potatoes into even sizes and boil in salted water until cooked. Drain and set aside 150ml of the water.

Place the potatoes and 100ml of the water back into the pan, then add the milk and double cream. Bring the ingredients to the boil and blend using a hand blender until the mixture reaches a smooth, velvety texture. Add more water if the mixture appears too thick.

Pass the now fully blended mixture through a fine sieve and if you have a cream whipper, pour in the mashed potato and charge with two gas chargers. Keep the mixture warm and set aside. If you do not have a cream whipper then just whip by hand but don't overwork.

For the mussels, place a deep tray on the stove and add the rice and tea leaves.

When the tray starts smoking, place a cooling rack on top of the tray and add the mussels, covering with foil and smoking for around 5 minutes.

Take the tray off the heat and replace with a saucepan, adding the cooked mussels and white wine. Place a lid on top of the saucepan and cook the mussels for a further 2 minutes.

Take the pan off the heat and pour the white wine and mussels into a deep bowl, covering with cling film to keep warm.

Begin cooking the fish by placing a non stick pan on the stove.

Add 1 tbsp of grapeseed oil and place the turbot into the pan. Season with salt and pepper.

After 2 minutes, add a tsp of butter and place into the oven for 4 minutes.

Take the fish out the oven and place on a warm plate.

Place the pan back onto the stove and add the wild mushrooms, sauté for 1 minute before adding in the smoked mussels, cucumber, capers and chopped dill.

Spoon the mixture over the fish.

If using the whipper, expel the potato foam and pour over the fish. If you are using a hand-blender, froth the sauce before pouring.

Finish with a few leaves of dill and serve.

The Show MUST GO ON

Hosting everything from dinners and conferences to large scale exhibitions, The Lincolnshire Showground places local produce at the heart of its event calendar.

The Lincolnshire Showground lives and breathes events; especially when it comes to good food. Hosting everything from dinners to conferences and exhibitions to large scale events, they strive to celebrate the very best of Lincolnshire, attracting agricultural communities, families, international guests and school children to engage, entertain and educate in the most lively and exciting way possible.

Located just four miles North of Lincoln city centre, the Lincolnshire Showground has a rather unique history thanks to The Lincolnshire Agricultural Society having had a strong presence in the county for years, carving Lincolnshire a well-established identity as one of the best and brightest farming communities, whilst working to continually preserve their natural landscape.

Growing and developing each year, this flourishing venue recognises that its Agricultural Society roots are the foundations of its success, and that it is becoming the ultimate meeting place for those who love to celebrate Lincolnshire.

The Lincolnshire Show

Held within the county by the Lincolnshire Agricultural Society since 1869, the Lincolnshire Show is one of the region's most significant dates in the calendar attracting over 60,000 people a year over two days in June each year. First hosted at the Lincolnshire Showground in 1959 after being held at various venues around the county, the event was by then in its 76th year and has only ever been called off on a handful of occasions in its 131 year history; largely due to the Second World War.

Boasting over 600 trade stands and a dedicated food court blossoming with produce, the Lincolnshire Show also provides entertainment, equine events, a look at livestock and agricultural machinery as well as a display of classic cars, children's educational activities, entertainment for all the family and a horticultural area which all fit for a fun-filled family day out.

Like many of the Lincolnshire Showground's projects, the Lincolnshire Show places celebrating local produce and education at the forefront of its objectives which further the welfare and progress of Lincolnshire's agricultural industry.

This colourful event has such a positive impact on the Lincolnshire community that it comes as no surprise that it is already gearing up to grow next year with even more ways to celebrate Lincolnshire's wonderful farming industry and the natural rolling surroundings in which it sits.

Lincolnshire Showground

Lincolnshire Food & Gift Fair

Held annually at the end of November, the Lincolnshire Food and Gift Fair is one of the most exciting events to take place at The Lincolnshire Showground.

Originally organised on a year where the Lincolnshire Show wasn't able to take place to give the Society's members, guests and regular visitors an opportunity to get together and celebrate local producers, the Food & Gift Fair has grown over the last 15 years to become a stand-out event in the Lincolnshire festive calendar.

Praising the food, drink and gifts made locally by the businesses and people of Lincolnshire, the fair has become a home for over 150 exhibitors who each bring their own individual talents to create an event where the festive spirit truly takes hold.

Taking place across two exhibition halls and all under one roof, the Lincolnshire Food & Gift Fair is seen by many as the perfect way to get in the Christmas spirit, soaking up the warm atmosphere whilst picking up a selection of gorgeous gifts and festive foods from all of their favourite local suppliers.

The event is filled with special attractions which entertain guests of all ages including choir group performances, cookery demonstrations from top local chefs and food producers and hands-on craft workshops to create Christmas gifts with a personal touch.

There are countless contributors lending their time and skills to the event as well as Lincolnshire foodie favourites such as Boston Sausage, Cote Hill Cheese, Duffy's Chocolates, Hope & Glory Coffee Co, Mr Huda's, Pipers Crisps and Pocklington's Bakery; many of which are known in the community for their distinctive local products.

The Lincolnshire Showground provides the perfect setting with lovingly crafted gifts and delicious products available around every corner of the popular two day event. The Lincolnshire Kitchen, the event's dedicated cookery demonstration area, has collaborated with the likes of Redhill Farm Free-range Pork and Uncle Henry's as well as a number of chefs from Lincolnshire's fantastic choice of local restaurants and even a few well-known TV personalities to give a taste of Lincolnshire to locals and visitors that will keep them coming back year after year.

The Lincolnshire Agricultural Society

The Lincolnshire Showground is the home of the Lincolnshire Agricultural Society, and has been since 1958 when the land was purchased to become a permanent venue for the popular Lincolnshire Show. Supporting and educating about food and farming in the county, the Lincolnshire Agricultural Society works hard to promote the benefits of a sustainable environment as well as bringing the community together.

Growing across 270 acres of land, the Showground has diversified over the years with a number of buildings including the Exhibition Hall, the Tennyson Pavilion, agricultural buildings, stable accommodation and the Epic Centre each becoming part of the project. The Epic Centre, officially opened in 2008, is an award-winning building and one of the greenest conference centres in the UK, catering for up to 1,200 people at a time in its spacious halls.

The generous expanse of land involved in the project gives fantastic opportunity for the Lincolnshire Showground to host a wide range of events alongside their own including equine shows, ceremonies and concerts as well as niche festivals and international rallies which draw visitors in their thousands to put Lincolnshire on the cultural and culinary map.

However, for the Agricultural Society, education is one of the key focuses of its chariatable objectives. Their annual 'Countryside Lincs' event serves as a fun family day out all about food, farming and countryside activites. Local schools have also become involved in their 'National Farmhouse Breakfast Week', 'Grown Your Own Potato' and 'Tractors into Schools' initiatives, giving children awareness of the part they play in Lincolnshire's rich farming community.

The 'Grow Your Own Potato' and 'Tractors Into Schools' initiatives the Showground get involved in also serve to make children conscious of the part they play in Lincolnshire's rich farming community. The Showground team arrange a number of trips to local producers for young farmers of the future and those interested in a career in the food industry to learn all about their home county. The prolific Lincolnshire Farming Conference also establishes the Agricultural Society's strong and ever-evolving community by inviting local farmers to network with speakers and exhibitors, building a tight knit society which really shows what Lincolnshire is all about.

Live and Let LIVESEY

Since taking the helm at The Livesey Arms in 2014, Rosie Dicker has combined her twin passions of food and art to create a distinctive dining experience.

Rosie Dicker has a career which dates back to the 1970s in which she has always sought out the best ingredients to create food which makes a lasting impression.

The Livesy Arms is a shining tribute to her expertise and knowledge, standing in the charming village of Ludborough, nestled between the historic market town of Louth and The Lincolnshire Wolds. Here, a strong, tight-knit team serve up quality dishes with promises of true hospitality.

Whilst the traditional English pub-style building is graciously aged, Rosie has helped to revamp the ancient little inn to a 21st century eatery, giving weary travellers a top quality dining experience with every visit.

Rosie, who grew up in Lincolnshire, began studying art at university before setting out to carve a distinguished career in restaurant management. After a break from the industry to raise her family, she returned to the work she loved when she launched her own catering business 'Rosie's Kitchen' which specialised in high-end catering for parties as well as a highly regarded supper club.

It was during this time that her exploits caught the attention of a local gentleman in Ludborough who'd recently purchased the The Livesy Arms to prevent it falling into disrepair. He wanted to recreate a sense of community in his village and Rosie was asked to get involved.

After previously running both a successful pub in Wainfleet and the popular Alfred's Restaurant in Louth, Rosie could hardly refuse a project that reflected two of her strengths so well. After working hard to create The Livesey Arms' beautiful state-of-the-art kitchen, in addition to influencing the design and overall feel of the newly renovated inn, she opened the doors for the first time in the summer of 2014.

Rosie has always been fortunate enough to be able to find and use the best ingredients of Lincolnshire, long before it became the norm. In fact, her ethos has always been to choose the best products and do the least with them. The Livesy Arms has since become a destination dining experience which continues to grow as one of Lincolnshire's best and most promising new establishments.

The food here has a strong connection to its Lincolnshire heritage as much as it does to Rosie's influences from art and nature. Inspired by the rolling green hills of the Lincolnshire Wolds and her eclectic eye for detail, Rosie's dishes are non-structured and beautifully laid out, which is a stark contrast to the minimalistic gourmet serving techniques you'll find in the city.

Her efforts won the venue the Journal's Restaurant of the Year title; not just for their food but for their young, highly trained team who Rosie insists on treating with the utmost respect and care that most establishments may overlook. Most recently, Rosie won the Lincolnshire Life's Chef of the Year competition. With their signature dry-aged Lincolnshire Josper grilled ribeye steak rapidly becoming their most recognisable dish, The Livesy Arms lives by consistency to bring guests fresh and lovingly crafted food which resonates long after leaving.

Livesey Arms

Livesey Arm's
HERB CRUSTED RACK OF LAMB & SHOULDER
with onion purée
This is a delicious warming winter dish showcasing some sublime local ingredients.

Ingredients

For the slow cooked shoulder

2kg shoulder of the best Lincolnshire lamb

Olive oil

Flaked salt

Black pepper

1 bulb unpeeled garlic cut across

3 pealed red onions

Sprig of marjoram

For the onion purée

2 tbsp butter

2 onions, sliced

4 cups chicken stock

Flaked salt

For the herb crusted rack of lamb

2 French trimmed racks of lamb, boned and stripped of sinew

Dijon mustard

300g breadcrumbs

300g parsley

2 tbsp fresh thyme

Olive oil

Butter

1 clove garlic

Salt and pepper

For the jus

½ pint homemade lamb stock

55g cold diced butter

Method

For the slow cooked shoulder

Preheat the oven to 170°C.

To begin cooking the lamb shoulder, lay the garlic, onions and marjoram in the bottom of a roasting tray and place the lamb shoulder on top. Rub the shoulder with olive oil and season liberally with salt and pepper.

Cover the tray tightly with foil and place in the oven.

Cook for 4 hours. When it is done the meat should pull apart with two forks easily.

Allow to cool then take the meat off the bone. Tightly roll in cling film.

For the onion purée

Heat the butter in a saucepan and add the sliced onions and flaked salt.

Place a lid on the pan and cook over a low heat until soft, making sure they don't colour.

Reduce the heat and add the stock, then cook for a further 5 minutes. Leave uncovered for 20 minutes.

Blend to a smooth purée and season as required.

For the herb crusted rack of lamb

Preheat the oven to 220°C.

Start by blending the breadcrumbs with the parsley, thyme, olive oil and garlic.

Brush the lamb with Dijon mustard and roll in the crust mixture liberally.

Heat the butter and olive oil in a frying pan over a high heat.

When the butter has melted, sear the lamb, colouring on all sides.

Season and transfer to a roasting tin.

Roast for 10 minutes until medium rare.

Allow to rest, keep warm.

For the jus

In a saucepan over a medium heat, reduce the stock then whisk in the diced butter to thicken.

To assemble, smear the onion purée on a warmed plate, add the slow cooked shoulder and the herb crusted rack of lamb and pour over some of the jus. Serve with your favourite winter vegetables.

Lincolnshire produce with ITALIAN FLAIR

Mario and Holly Cantelmi offer the best local Lincolnshire produce
and pair this with inspiration from the Italian Amalfi coast.

This is not the first time that Mario Cantelmi has brought delicious Italian dishes to the UK, but it is a first for family-run Lincolnshire restaurant Mario's which he opened with his wife Holly just under a year ago.

Hailing from the South of Italy near the Amalfi coast, Mario's father Pasquale arrived in the UK back in 1982 and began running restaurants including Sheffield's ever-popular La Terrazza in 1997.

Mario learned his father's trade from an early age; from polishing cutlery and mopping the floors at just 10-years-old to becoming a chef at 16. Today he is head chef in his very own business and has successfully built a relaxed, cosmopolitan eatery with his wife Holly, who he met when they both worked at his father's restaurant as teenagers.

Mario's of course has its own unique spin on the Italian classic dishes that Mario was taught to perfection whilst also picking up his father's ability to adopt local resources to create a delicious, versatile Italian menu. Mario picks up all of their ingredients locally from Lincolnshire including meat from the nearby butchery and fresh fish from Grimsby, whilst their specialist beer is imported directly from Amalfi for a truly traditional Italian touch. However, it is the vegetables grown in Lincolnshire's own soil that make Mario's Italian inspired dishes taste out of this world, with their undisputed freshness and flavour. As anyone who has travelled and tasted will know, pasta dishes and pizza are just the tip of the iceberg when it comes to delicious Italian cooking.

Using old school Mediterranean-style ingredients, Mario's create dishes which are unique to every customer, with each item on the menu being made to order to the diner's own taste. This dexterity and initiative in the kitchen is what makes Mario's stand out alongside their friendly, welcoming family atmosphere.

Holly's own parents were small business owners and her passion for an authentic Italian experience with a Lincolnshire spin is strongly shared with her husband and their staff. Although new, the dedicated team at Mario's are well-rehearsed in providing an excellent dining experience and for this reason, Mario's is one of the most exciting venues in Lincolnshire.

Mario's

Mario's
RISOTTO MARIO

Serves one

Ingredients

125g Arborio rice

100ml double cream

80g chicken, diced

5 fresh scallops

50g garden peas

1 garlic clove

2 tbsp olive oil

30g white onion, finely chopped

200ml vegetable stock

Sprig of fresh parsley

Sprig of fresh dill

1 glass of white wine

Salt and pepper

Method

Heat the olive oil in a pan then add garlic and onion to fry.

Add the diced chicken to the pan and sear it, adding a dash of white wine.

Add the rice to the pan, pouring in the stock a little at a time, stirring until it simmers.

Place the fresh scallops and peas into the pan and stir into the risotto.

Sprinkle the mixture with flat leaf parsley and a stem of fresh dill.

Pour in the cream and reduce until the risotto mixture becomes sticky. If the risotto is still not quite cooked, keeping adding more stock until it reaches the desired sticky consistency.

Season with salt and pepper to your liking.

Earned his CHOPS

Born and raised on the farm, Jim Sutcliffe is passionate about maintaining the heritage of Lincolnshire rare breeds.

Located in the historic market town of Louth, Meridian Meats is the beloved family butcher's shop owned by Jim Sutcliffe, a Lincolnshire-born local lad who won BBC Butcher of The Year in 2009.

Jim was raised in the heart of the Lincolnshire Wolds on his parents farm. It was there his passion for rare breeds began with their Longhorn cattle. Jim's parents started keeping Longhorns in 1993 when they were still on the Rare Breeds Survival Trust's "watch list" and they soon became the mainstay of the farm. For them to be profitable an outlet was needed for the beef as well as the pedegee livestock and Meridian Meats was born, selling their rare breed beef direct from the farm and so called because the farm is situated on the Greenwich meridian, initially located in a mobile shop in the farmyard.

Jim who had learned his farming and breeding expertise first hand on the farm, set out to earn his butchery skills with "Britain's Best Butcher" Eric Phipps from Mareham le Fen. Eric offered Jim an apprenticeship after he wrote to him showing a strong interest in the trade, and he sought to teach him everything from slaughtering to rendering lard and preparation. It was when Eric retired in 2005 that Jim felt an urge to seize the opportunity to put his skills to work with their own meat back on the farm at Meridian Meats. In 2008

demand outstripped supply and Meridian Meats relocated a few miles north on the Meridian line to the Georgian market town of Louth. Here things went from strength to strength with them becoming the centre of a revival in hearty old-fashioned English cooking. Selling a selection of succulent home-produced meats including the beef of Lincoln Reds, cross bred rare breed lamb, Lincolnshire pork and of course, the Longhorn beef, which scooped Meridian Meats the title of 'Britain's Best Steak' in 2009.

Specialising in traditional Lincolnshire products such as stuffed chine, haslet and Lincolnshire sausage, making them all by hand, Jim considers the methods for such delicacies as a 'dying art'. But he has learnt to perfect each one of them, making a name for himself both within and outside of Lincolnshire

Jim is very patriotic when it comes to his home county and keeps the spirit of Lincolnshire's agricultural history alive with his knowledge and enthusiasm for his work. Earning several Great Taste Awards for his specialist sausages; some recipes of which include curried goat; beef and sweet chilli; pork pear and Stilton and beef thyme and wholegrain mustard, Jim continues to collect local, national and international accolades'.

Homemade
Pork Pie

Lincolnshire Wolds
Lamb Loin Chops

Meridian Meats
Best Lincolnshire
Sausages
More seasoned, multi GOLD award
winners! 85% Min meat
£8.50/kg   £3.84/lb
CONTAINS PRESERVATIVE

Meridian Meats
LINCOLNSHIRE PIGS' FRY

Serves 4.

Ingredients

For the fry:

300g pork, diced

100g pigs liver, sliced

100g pigs kidney, diced

2 medium onions, sliced

1 clove of garlic, crushed

1 large cooking apple, cored and chopped

Handful of fresh sage leaves, chopped Save one-third for the dumplings

1 litre stock, pork if possible

Lincolnshire rapeseed oil

2 tbsp plain flour

Sea salt and black pepper

For the dumplings:

100g self-raising flour

50g beef suet

4-5 tbsp cold water

Chopped sage leaves, saved from the fry

For the mashed potatoes:

3-4 potatoes, use a good mashing variety such as Désirée

200g salted butter

50ml double cream

Sea salt and black pepper

Method

Heat a glug of rapeseed oil in a large ovenproof casserole dish with a lid and sweat the onions and garlic gently without browning.

Whilst the onions sweat, put 2 tablespoons of plain flour into a large plastic bag and season with salt and pepper.

Place the diced pork, liver and kidney into the bag, holding the top tightly before shaking well to coat the contents.

Remove the softened onions from the pan.

Turn the heat up, adding a little more oil if necessary, brown your floured meat.

Add the onions, along with the apple, the stock, two-thirds of the sage leaves and a season of salt and pepper.

Put the lid onto your casserole dish and place into a low oven, the bottom oven if using an Aga or set at 140°C.

Cook for 3-4 hours.

Once your pigs' fry is cooked, begin to make the dumplings and mash.

Start by preparing your potatoes. Peel and dice into 2 inch pieces. Steam them until soft for 20-30 minutes.

To make your dumplings add the flour, suet, remaining sage, and water to a bowl, with a pinch of salt.

Mix the ingredients to form a dough.

Divide the dough into 8 and gently form into small balls with floured hands.

Place the dumplings on top of the simmering fry, replace the lid and return to a hot oven at 180-200°C for 20-25 minutes.

For the final 5 minutes remove the lid to allow the dumplings to crisp.

Whilst the dumplings finish cooking in the oven, drain the potatoes and mash, adding the butter and cream until smooth.

Season generously with salt and pepper.

Once your dumplings are well risen and crisp, you are ready to serve.

Original
AND BEST

The Original Cake Company have been baking cakes since 1972 and these days supply some of the the UK's biggest retailers.

Working with cakes all day might sound like a dream job to many and for the staff at The Original Cake Company, it kind of is.

From humble beginnings baking cakes in a kitchen at home for local fairs and enjoyment, The Original Cake Company has been working to create traditional handmade cakes since 1972. Their staff and location may have changed, but their ethos remains the same.

The Original Cake Company has been the name behind some of Britain's finest cakes for over four decades. They continue to bake delicious, handmade cakes for a number of farm shops and local businesses, as well as independent specialist retailers across the UK. You may have also unwittingly sampled their delightful recipes in John Lewis' festive hampers as well as other select premium retailers for which their moreish cakes are supplied. Who else would bake cakes that have been served in the House of Commons than this growing Lincolnshire gem?

From their signature fruit and speciality Christmas cakes to their chocolate truffle cakes and flapjacks, The Original Cake Company have perfected each recipe in-house throughout the decades, with their small team of experienced bakers who have around 150 years of experience between them. They create and decorate all of their products in small batches entirely by hand before sending out to some of their local and national customers. They have worked with the nearby Doddington Hall to launch a range of products, becoming their flagship seller whilst their granola flapjacks have even bagged them a Great Taste Award.

Unique due to their artisan methods, everyone who works at The Original Cake Company has a loyal passion for their product and believes in the quality of the cakes they sell. Simon Woodwiss, the Managing Director, has been helping to build the team, recruiting the most talented folk in their respective fields; something which certainly shines through in the quality of their cakes. Their marketing whizz Gemma Hawker who jumped feet first into the company just under a year ago is keen to point out that; 'It's not hard to sell something you to truly love.'

Packaged with a hand-crafted feel to reflect their roots, The Original Cake Company are not just a local favourite in their home county of Lincolnshire but are winning fans across the UK each year. Their secret ingredient is obvious; the pride each member of their team takes to create their fantastic, traditional cakes is what makes this company truly special and they continue to spread the word far and wide.

The Original Cake Co.
BRANDY, FRUIT & NUT LOAF CAKE

Proving that fruit cake is not just for Christmas, this special brandy, fruit and nut loaf cake is The Original Cake Company's specialist recipe. Rich, fruity and moist, it's the perfect addition to any dining table or tea party. Serves 6-8.

Ingredients

500g sultanas

75g glace cherries, cut into chunks

100ml of brandy

85g softened butter

100g soft brown sugar

1 tbsp of black treacle

100g plain flour sifted with ½ tsp mixed spice and 2 tsp baking powder

2 medium eggs

30g chopped walnuts

For the topping:

12 whole glace cherries

8 walnut halves

40g whole blanched almonds

Method

Makes 2 loaves. One for now and one for later or to give to a friend!

Soak the sultanas and cherries in the brandy overnight.

Heat the oven to 160°C and line two 1lb loaf tins with greaseproof paper.

Cream the butter and sugar in a bowl together until light and fluffy. Stir in the black treacle. Gradually add the eggs along with a little of the flour mixture.

Fold in the remaining flour mixture.

Gently stir in the walnuts and soaked fruits, along with any of the remaining liquid, until fully incorporated into the mix to create a batter.

Spoon the batter into the two prepared loaf tins and level the top of the cake with the back of a spoon. Top the cakes with the cherries and nuts.

You may need to cover the tops of the cakes with foil during baking to prevent over browning on the top of the cake.

Bake the cakes in the oven for around 1 hour or until they are firm to touch. Insert a fine skewer into the cake to see if it comes out clean.

Leave the cakes in the tins for 30 minutes before removing and cooling on a wire rack.

Once cool, the cakes can be stored in an airtight container.

The best way to serve is to slice with a serrated edge knife, using a sawing action and wiping the blade with every cut before plating.

High FLYERS

With a rich history steeped in wartime folklore and an even brighter future on the horizon, the award-winning Petwood Hotel is a Lincolnshire gem dedicated to seasonal cooking and local provenance.

Lincolnshire's associated history with the RAF is well documented, earning its nickname as 'The Bomber County', but one local dining destination remains a nostalgic landmark to this chapter in history. The Petwood Hotel is a beautiful turn of the century estate located in the stunning grounds of Woodhall Spa. It stands today as an award-winning hotel and restaurant which draws in visitors for its delightful food, scenic Edwardian-style gardens and fascinating history.

A private home until 1933, The Petwood Hotel was expanded by architect Frank Peck with a 'Tudor to Jacobean' style facade. It is perhaps best known for being home to the RAF's 617 'Dambusters' Squadron who were stationed at the hotel after it was requisitioned during the Second World War as an Officer's Mess. The ultimate poster boys moved in during January 1944 after the 97 and 619 Squadrons moved out. They would fly out for missions from the nearby airfield, returning afterwards for a drink in what is today the Squadron Bar.

Located just off the main dining room, it has become a wonderfully sentimental tourist attraction for those interested in Britain's wartime history. Over the bar today you can find the branch of a tree which was impaled in the fuselage of a Lancaster Bomber during one of the 617 missions; a token piece of memorabilia which helps to make Petwood such a unique and special location.

Featuring a traditional interior with an ornate staircase and 30 acres of beautiful surrounding garden and woodlands, the hotel is the perfect escape. Regularly hosting weddings and special events, the Petwood Hotel has been celebrated for the excellent menus and hospitality, promoting the Lincolnshire provenance of the best locally-sourced ingredients, including a hand-chosen wine list and local line up of real ales.

Head chef Philip Long joined the team in 2013 after years working in London, including at spell at Claridges. He has created a varied and seasonal menu for the Dining Room and Terrace Bar as well as training young chefs who have found Petwood to be the perfect springboard for their careers.

Awarded Hotel of The Year at the Select Lincolnshire Food, Drink and Hospitality Awards in 2014 as well as star ratings from AA and Visit England, it comes as no surprise that Petwood's friendly staff and relaxed atmosphere allows guests to feel as if they are being welcomed into a familiar family home.

Whether enjoying their Sunday lunch or an evening meal prepared with the freshest Lincolnshire ingredients, diners can enjoy Cote Hill's local cheeses, Walker and Walker's flavoursome Lincolnshire sausages and fresh fish from Grimsby; presented with a homely Petwood twist.

Petwood Hotel's
CANNON OF VENISON WITH PEA PURÉE

The rich meaty venison works well with the sharpness of the redcurrants.
Serves 4.

Ingredients

4x185g venison cannon

500g peas

60g shallots

40g unsalted butter

250g redcurrant jelly

1 punnet of redcurrants

640g mashed potato

4 egg yolks

200g venison liver

500ml red wine

100ml Port

1 litre of veal or beef stock

Method

Melt the unsalted butter in a pan and add the chopped shallots, cooking until they are clear, without colour.

Meanwhile begin cooking the peas in boiling salted water until tender and drain.

When both the peas and shallots are cooked, blend them together in a food processor and pass through a sieve for a smooth consistency. Keep warm and set aside.

For the sauce you will need to start by reducing the red wine, port and stock with the redcurrant jelly in a pan until the sauce is a slightly sticky consistency. Set this aside and also keep hot.

For the potato nest, mix the mashed potato with the egg yolk and beat together well, seasoning to taste.

Once smooth, transfer the potato to a piping bag and use a star nozzle to pipe the potato into four nest shapes onto a parchment lined baking sheet.

Place in the oven for 10 minutes until the potato turns golden brown

To begin cooking the venison cannon, heat a frying pan with a little rapeseed oil, until the oil is hot.

Dry the cannons well in a disposable kitchen cloth before carefully adding the cannons to the pan.

Roll each cannon until all sides are sealed.

Place your now seared cannons in the hot oven to cook for a further 6 minutes.

Once cooked, take out of the pan and place on a warm plate to rest.

Next dice the liver into smaller pieces and cook in the same already-heated pan and oil used for the cannons for about 2-3 minutes.

Once cooked, drain and add some redcurrants and a small amount of sauce.

To assemble begin to plate up the dish by putting some sauce in the centre of the warmed dinner plate, before adding the potato nest, filling this with the liver and redcurrant mix.

Using two serving spoons to quenelle the pea purée and then add to the plate.

Cut the rare cooked cannon in half and arrange between the potato and pea purée, garnishing with the remaining redcurrants and baby watercress to serve.

Rachel Green's
BRITISH VENISON LOIN

with herb and mustard crust and autumn berry compote

Rachel Green has appeared on TV shows such as Yorkshire TV's Flying Cook,
Kill It! Cook It! Eat it! on BBC3 and Farm of Fussy Eaters on UK TV Style.
Serves four.

Ingredients

4 venison loin (approx. 200g)

Sea salt and black pepper

4 tbsp rapeseed oil

30g butter

For the herb crust:

4 tsp Dijon mustard

3 tbsp softened unsalted butter

100g fresh white breadcrumbs

A large handful finely chopped parsley leaves

2 tbsp fresh rosemary leaves, chopped

1 tbsp fresh thyme leaves, chopped

Sea salt and black pepper

For the new potatoes:

400g baby new potatoes

2 springs fresh thyme

A few cloves garlic, peeled and crushed

2 tbsp rapeseed oil

30g butter

For the autumn berry compote:

500g autumn berries including blackberries, mulberries and myrtle berries,

6 crushed juniper berries

1 star anise (optional)

Zest and juice of one small orange

2 tbsp runny English honey

Method

Preheat oven to 200°C

For the potatoes, cut them in half length-ways and par boil for 8 minutes, drain and cool slightly.

Put the potatoes into a bowl and toss with the oil, thyme, garlic, sea salt and black pepper.

In a roasting tray, melt the butter. Roast the potatoes for approximately 40-50 minutes, until golden brown.

Meanwhile, begin preparing the venison loin by seasoning generously with sea salt and black pepper.

Mix the mustard and softened butter to form a paste.

Mix the breadcrumbs, parsley, rosemary and thyme together.

Spread the butter paste over each side of the loin, and then press the loins in the breadcrumb mixture, coating each side well.

Heat a pan with 4 tablespoons of rapeseed oil and 30g of butter. When the oil and butter is hot, seal the venison on both sides until the surface is golden brown this should take no longer than 1 minute on each side.

Place the venison in the oven on top of the roast potatoes after the potatoes have been cooking for around 45 minutes and cook the venison for 3-5 minutes until the meat is rare.

Remove the venison loin and potatoes from the oven, allowing to rest for 5 minutes in a warm place. Slice the venison.

Place the potatoes in the middle of a large warmed platter and lay the venison on top.

Serve with the autumn compote in a jug.

Autumn berry compote

Put all the ingredients into a pan and simmer gently for 2 minutes or until the fruit releases its juice slightly.

Serve with the venison and potatoes.

Rachel Green's
CHOCOLATE MOUSSE CAKE

Rachel shares her delectable chocolate mousse cake recipe. Serves 12.

Ingredients

25g cocoa powder

2 tbsp boiling water

100g caster sugar

100g self-raising flour

1 tsp baking powder

2 eggs

100g butter

2 tbsp brandy

For the mousse:

300g plain chocolate

450ml whipping cream

To serve:

225g raspberries and blueberries

Double cream, to serve

Cocoa powder, for dusting

Icing sugar, for dusting

Method

Grease a 20cm cake tin and line with baking paper. Preheat the oven to 180°C.

Put the cocoa powder into a large bowl, add the water and mix to a paste. Add the rest of the ingredients except for the brandy and beat until smooth. Spoon the mixture into the cake tin and level the surface. Bake in the oven for 20-25 minutes, or until a skewer inserted into the centre of the cake comes out clean.

While the cake is still hot, brush the top with brandy and leave to cool.

To make the mousse; break the chocolate into squares and place in a bowl. Melt over a pan of gently simmering water. Stir continuously; take care not to let the chocolate get too hot. Set aside to cool. Whip the cream until it forms soft peaks. Carefully fold the cream into the melted chocolate until smooth.

When the cake is cooled and still in the tin, spoon the mousse on top and level with a palette knife. Cover the cake tin in cling film and chill in the fridge overnight, until the mousse is firm.

To serve, remove the cake from the tin and transfer to a plate. Dust with cocoa powder and place the raspberries and blueberries in the centre. Serve with a dusting of icing sugar and a dollop of cream.

Home of the PRIZE PIGS

There's nowhere better in Lincolnshire than Redhill Farm to provide some of the finest free-range pork in the country.

Farmers, Jane and Terry Tomlinson, set out 18 years ago to provide the people in Lincolnshire with access to the best tasting, highest quality free-range pork straight from the people who produce it. The key to what they do well is giving their pigs everything they need but, just as importantly, nothing they don't need. They commit the extra time, effort, skill and expense needed to produce something of quality instead making things faster, easier and cheaper at the expense of quality.

Ethically farmed, reared and produced to the highest standards possible, the free-range pork at Redhill Farm is of exceptional quality, which is why it has become Lincolnshire's go-to for local businesses and restaurants as well as loyal customers. Producing everything from matured, cured and smoked bacon and hams to traditional Lincolnshire Sausages and Haslets, hand-raised pork pies and black pudding as well as their free-range pork; the proof is found in the queues at Farmers' Markets and the listings on menus around the county and across the UK.

All of Redhill Farm's free-range pork comes from their own herd of Duroc cross Landrace pigs which roam freely, wallowing and rooting around in the sandy soil at the farm, attracting interest from passers-by and visitors to the Farm Shop. The Farm Shop also sells their own grass-fed beef and lamb, eggs from their free-range chickens as well as a selection of the best examples of other local and regional food.

Having been regular stall-holders at farmers' markets for the past 15 years it comes as no surprise that word has spread beyond Lincolnshire, earning Redhill Farm an astounding number of national awards as wells as many fans, becoming suppliers to Jamie Oliver and James Martin and sending pork pies to Lords' Cricket Ground. Their products have consistently scooped countless 1, 2 and 3 Star Gold's at the Great Taste Awards for over 10 years running including winning the 'Fine Food Oscar' for the region in 2014. Episodes of BBC's Countryfile and James Martin's Food Map of Britain were filmed at the farm and they have been named as one of the Top 3 Artisan Producers by BBC Good Food Magazine and one of the Top 5 Bacon Curers by the Financial Times food writer.

Although Redhill Farm have received prestigious national awards and recognition and supply high profile chefs around the UK they remain selective about the businesses they supply and continue to choose to sell most of what they produce in person at local farmers' markets and in their farm shop. This ensures that they can remain an ethical small business that values their customers and concentrates on quality from farming through to retail.

Redhill Farm Free Range Pork
BLACK PUDDING STUFFED FILLET

Made using Redhill Farm's free-range pork. This recipe merges their delicious tenderloin pork fillet with black pudding and oak smoked bacon.

Serves 4.

Ingredients

Use a 'Redhill Farm Black Pudding Stuffed Fillet Recipe Kit'

Kit includes:

300-400g free-range pork tenderloin fillet

200g Redhill Farm oak smoked streaky bacon or pancetta

250g Redhill Farm black pudding

Method

Remove the rind from the oak smoked streaky bacon and lay out on a board in strips from left to right, just barely overlapping to form a sheet.

Slice your pork fillet lengthways to open it out but not cut through.

Take your black pudding and begin stuffing into the middle in a long sausage-shape. Form the fillet around the stuffing to close up as much as possible.

Place the stuffed fillet on one side of the bacon sheet and gently roll the bacon up around the fillet.

Tie with string in three places to secure the fillet and its' stuffing.

Place on a baking tray with the overlapping edges of the bacon face down and roast for 40 minutes at 180°C until the bacon is golden and crispy.

Remove from oven and leave to rest.

Make a jus to accompany your stuffed fillet with the scrapings from the pan using wine or stock reduction.

Serve thinly sliced with seasonal vegetables.

Love at FIRST BITE

She's a baker ... he's a butcher ...
the rest is a tale of food perfection baked in harmony.

They say you can find love in the strangest of places and for some, those places can be a little stranger than others. Sadie and Russell Hirst met the same year Russell, a butcher with over 30 years of experience, opened up his shop RJ Hirst Butchers in 2003. Sadie was a fifth generation baker who made a chance visit and following that first fleeting moment, the pair discovered their mutual passion for food, becoming partners in both life and business.

Specialising in traditional Lincolnshire dishes using only the best artisan ingredients, Russell and Sadie do everything the old fashioned way including hand-making their own famous Lincolnshire sausages and pork pies, as well as selling high quality local produce such as cakes, pastries, free-range eggs and plum loaf.

Treasured by locals, RJ Hirst Butchers are an award-winning business who still remain a favourite at the heart of their community thanks to their labour of love in creating food that can truly be enjoyed.

RJ Hirst Family Butchers
LINCOLNSHIRE SAUSAGE & ONION PLAIT

This is a delicious hearty dish, which uses local Lincolnshire ingredients. Versatile and wholesome, the dish can be eaten hot as part of a main meal or cold and sliced. It also makes a great addition to a buffet as it yields generous portions and the delicate plaiting of pastry is an impressive sight to behold.

Ingredients

500g Curtis of Lincoln quality puff pastry

800g RJ Hirst Lincolnshire sausage meat

2 Fairburns local free-range eggs, lightly beaten

1 jar onion marmalade

Method

Begin by lining a large baking tray with two layers of baking parchment and preheat the oven to 200°C.

Cut your puff pastry block in half and roll each section out until 40cm long x 20cm wide.

Divide the sausage meat into four sections.

Add a layer of sausage meat along the centre of your pastry rectangles leaving a 3cm gap from the top and bottom and a 4cm gap on either side.

Spoon on half a jar of the onion marmalade and spread all over the sausage meat.

Add the remaining halves of the sausage meat on top of the marmalade to create a second layer.

Make downwards sloping cuts about 1cm apart along the pastry on either side of the meat. You should be able to get 14 cuts on either side.

Brush the beaten egg mixture all over the pastry.

Starting at the top, fold down the pastry over the meat filling and then alternately fold the strips over to create a plait, working your way down to the bottom. Finish by folding the bottom over the remaining meat to seal neatly.

Repeat with the second plait and then carefully lift both plaits onto your lined tray.

Glaze all over with your beaten egg to get a golden brown finish in the oven.

Bake for 45 minutes to 1 hour until pastry is golden and puffed up and meat is cooked thoroughly.

Mediterranean Passion in LINCOLNSHIRE

The rustic tastes of the Mediterranean, combined with luxury boutique accommodation... San Pietro is a must visit Lincolnshire destination.

When it comes to destination dining in Lincolnshire, San Pietro takes the title for most innovative and unusual. An award-winning family owned restaurant, wedding venue and hotel, San Pietro is situated in Scunthorpe and housed inside a stunning Grade II listed 18th century windmill with a luxurious boutique-style interior. Decorated with original and rejuvenated 1940s furniture and unique textile pieces, the elegant ambience is not the only thing to write home about during your stay. Owned by Michelle and Pietro Catalano, the two made a formidable team when pairing Michelle's background in interior design with Pietro's exquisite Mediterranean cooking to create a restaurant experience that has won them a number of prestigious accolades since they opened 2003.

Sicilian born Pietro's passion for cooking food comes from generations of his family and his mother, where home was always full of fresh produce and sourcing the finest ingredients. For the past 10 years Pietro has worked tirelessly alongside 2-Star Michelin pedigree head chef Christopher Grist to create a menu that takes the best ingredients of Lincolnshire to concoct delicious French, Spanish and Italian inspired artisan dishes.

Whether they are putting a Mediterranean finesse on historic Lincolnshire favourites like rabbit to combining Italian classic desserts with Lincolnshire baked pastries, San Pietro is foodie heaven for those who wish to try something exciting and different. With regular menu changes, attentive service and locally-sourced produce, San Pietro also houses over 115 wines from across the globe and hosts a candle-lit private dining room for lucky guests who choose to plan their special event with the San Pietro team.

Despite only opening the upper rooms of the building to become a hotel in 2014, San Pietro have already won awards for 'Funkiest B&B', a Gold Star rating for their accommodation and are highly lauded on TripAdvisor. These accolades sit comfortably besides their 2 AA Rosette Award for Culinary Excellence, a three-time win as Lincolnshire Journals' 'Restaurant Of The Year' and their name a regular feature in the Michelin Guide.

There's heart and soul to be found at San Pietro, both in the homely Lincolnshire setting and rustic Mediterranean food which caters for everyone from the corporate traveller to the culinarily adventurous family. Handmade from starter to the dessert, San Pietro's expertise lies in reflecting the old fashioned heritage of the county... with a warm-breeze blowing in from the Med.

San Pietro

San Pietro
ELEMENTS OF RABBIT & CARROT

As we all know, rabbits love carrots so what better accompaniment to rabbit than fresh Lincolnshire carrots cooked in a number of ways?

Ingredients

For the rabbit loin:

Fresh rabbit loin, trimmed

Sesame oil

Black sesame seeds

Salt and pepper

Butter

For the rabbit bob bon:

For the pane:

Panko breadcrumbs

Maldon salt

Ground black pepper

Dried rosemary

For the rabbit mousse:

100g diced seasoned rabbit meat

75ml double cream

1 whole egg

1 tsp fresh, diced rosemary

For the carrot purée:

12 carrots

½ tsp ground pepper

2 tsp salt

500ml water

3 tbsp Ultratex (available from health food shops)

For the carrot relish:

5 carrots, sliced julienne style

1 onion, finely diced

2 cloves garlic, sliced

Small bunch fresh thyme

2 lemons, zested and juiced

3 tbsp wholegrain mustard

100ml white wine

2 tsp Maldon salt

½ tsp ground black pepper

Method

For the rabbit loin

Roll the loin in the oil and season, then roll in sesame seeds.

Place the loin into hot pan and sear for approximately 1-2 minutes on both sides, coating the meat in butter.

For the rabbit bob bon

To make the rabbit bon bon, you'll need to make a rabbit mousse and a pane. Start by blitzing the rabbit meat and herbs in a food processor to a paste.

Add the egg into the mixture and continue to blend before adding cream.

Pipe onto a tray to required size and set in freezer for 15 minutes. Form into bon bon shape, mix the ingredients for the pane together and cover each mousse with the pane mix before setting aside to serve later.

For the carrot purée

Blitz ingredients together until puréed. Taste for seasoning and pour into a fine sieve allowing liquid to drain through.

Place the now smooth purée on heat to reduce; 750ml of carrot water should reduce by half using Ultratex.

For the carrot relish

Sweat the onions garlic, thyme and lemon zest in oil in a pan.

Add the carrots and sweat for 10 minutes, whilst adding seasoning.

Add the mustard and deglaze with the white wine and a squeeze of lemon juice. Cook ingredients on a low heat for 30 minutes. Cool to serve.

Deep fry the bon bon until golden. Decorate the plate with baby heritage carrots and serve with the carrot purée, relish and rabbit loin.

San Pietro
LOBSTER LINGUINE

This is a rich, luxurious yet simple dish which showcases ingredients to reflect the heart of Italian cooking. Serves 6.

Ingredients

550g linguine pasta

Extra virgin olive oil

3 lobsters, boiled prepped and cleaned (vacuum frozen raw lobsters can also be used)

250g baby plum tomatoes, washed and quartered

3 cloves of garlic, finely sliced

½ deseeded red chilli, finely chopped

30g cold salted butter, halved

Flat leaf parsley

Salt and pepper

Method

Heat a pan of salted water to a rolling boil.

Once all the fresh ingredients have been prepared, add the pasta to the hot water.

While the pasta begins to cook, heat a large frying pan with good quality olive oil.

Add the lobster shells and roast in the frying pan to impart flavour.

Throw in the sliced garlic and chilli and gently sauté to soften, taking care not over colour the garlic.

Place the quartered tomatoes in the pan and allow to cook, adding the lobster pieces and head meat into the mix; gently warm through.

Add half of the butter and parsley to emulsify the sauce.

Drain the pasta approximately 2 minutes before the finished cooking time and then add to the pan; retaining some of the salted pasta water for later.

Simmer the pasta in the lobster sauce, tossing the pan gently.

Add a small ladle of the pasta water - the starch will help to give a creamy consistency to the sauce.

Keep tossing the pan gently and place the final half of butter into the contents of the pan.

Check the seasoning and serve on a warmed plate, garnished with the claw meat and retained pieces of shell.

San Pietro
LIQUORICE PANNA COTTA

and cardamom choux with pink grapefruit sorbet.

A classic Italian dessert taken to another level with a Lincolnshire infusion.
Makes 8 small panna cotta.

Ingredients

For the panna cotta:

1 pint double cream

60g caster sugar

2 gelatine leaves

Liquorice stick

For the choux pastry:

250ml water

125g butter

140g flour

4-5 eggs, beaten

Flour, for dusting

For the cardamom crème pâtissière:

500ml milk

6 cardamom pods, cracked

1 vanilla pod, sliced in half

6 egg yolks

125g caster sugar

30g flour

15g corn flour

For the pink grapefruit sorbet:

500g pink grapefruit

500g caster sugar

600ml water

Lemon juice, to taste

Method

Soak gelatine leaves in cold water until soft and pliable.

Pour cream and liquorice in a pan and bring to a light boil until the liquorice is dissolved.

Leave to cool and infuse, covering with cling film.

Reheat and add caster sugar and soaked gelatine, whisking the ingredients into the boiled cream.

Pour into moulds and chill for at least 2 hours.

To begin making your choux pastry, heat the water and bring to the boil.

Mix in the flour and place into a mixer, adding the beaten eggs slowly one by one.

On a slow speed, incorporate each egg, allowing them to fully blend into the mixture.

The mixture should then be placed into a piping bag, ready to be piped to the desired shape and size.

To cook, have a pot of water handy and set the oven to 180°C degrees.

Pipe onto a baking tray (either papered or buttered) and add flour, leaving a reasonable distance between each pastry.

Place in the oven for 14-15 minutes. You must not open the oven once cooking has commenced. Once the pastries are cooked, look for a golden colour and test that they crack open.

Leave to cool and then pierce each pastry, ready to be filled.

For the cardamom crème pâtissière you will need to bring milk, cardamom pods and vanilla to scalding point.

Cling film and leave to infuse for 40 minutes whilst preparing the egg yolks, caster sugar, flour and corn flour by creaming together in a bowl.

Reheat the milk mixture and strain over the creamed egg mix before whisking together.

Place over a boiling bain marie and whisk further until the mixture thickens.

Leave to cook on a moderate heat for 20 minutes.

Mix all of the remaining ingredients for the pink grapefruit sorbet together.

Blitz in a food processor and pass through a fine sieve.

Churn mixture until ready and then place into the freezer for later.

Plate up panna cotta, pâtissière and choux pastry with the pink grapefruit sorbet adding a Pink grapefruit salad to garnish and serve.

Welcoming
AND LOCAL

Rustic charm, delicious food and a warm welcome
– The Stag Inn truly has it all.

A rustic inn with a homely family feel, The Stag Inn acquires its atmosphere from its licencees Mike and Samantha Loveridge, who run the pub and restaurant with the help of their son and twin daughters.

Creating wholesome and traditional English food made with the highest quality Lincolnshire ingredients, Mike brought his experience from years working as a Head Executive Chef in a hotel before buying the country village pub just under two years ago, making it the home of his very own eatery.

This 200-year-old stone built building has a classical old English pub feel with its flagstone flooring, wooden oak beams and roaring fire, which is perfectly complemented by the intimate and welcoming service of The Stag Inn's small and dedicated team.

Located just four miles from Mike and Samantha's family home, this small but inviting tavern even became a runner up for a Best Food award within just three months of opening.

The team at The Stag Inn strongly believe in local sustainability which is why they pick up all of their fish, vegetables and meat from neighbouring suppliers, using local cheeses and fruits for flavours which are utterly unique to Grantham.

Piecing together an à la carte menu which changes seasonally as well as delectable daily specials and pub classics such as steak and ale pies, The Stag Inn is a wonderful rest stop for those who seek a hearty meal with a cosy, comfortable ambience.

The Stag Inn

The Stag Inn
CHICKEN LIVER & THYME PÂTÉ

A refined and sophisticated starter with the best flavours of Lincolnshire.
Serves 4-6 people.

Ingredients

400g of chicken livers

4 banana shallots, finely sliced

400g salted butter

3 cloves of garlic, crushed

20g chopped fresh thyme

175ml red wine

50ml brandy

Sea salt and cracked black pepper to taste

Method

In a large frying pan or roasting tin, gently heat 100g of the butter.

Add the shallots, garlic, livers and thyme to the heated pan and cook while constantly stirring until the ingredients become soft and the livers are cooked through.

Add the brandy and flame until the alcohol has cooked off.

Pour the red wine into the mixture and season to taste.

Add 250g of the remaining butter in diced cubes, turning off the heat to stir the butter constantly until it has melted.

Pour the mixture into a large bowl and blend until smooth, creating your pâté.

Press the pâté through a fine sieve into your serving dish or individual ramekins.

Leave the pâté to chill for 1 hour before pouring the last 50g of melted butter over the top of the pâté.

Place your pâté in the fridge to cool for at least three hours before removing later on to serve.

The Stag Inn
SWEET RED ONION & TOMATO CHUTNEY

This sweet and savoury chutney is the perfect accompaniment to any dish with
a fruity tomato flavour and sharp red onion infusion. Makes 4-6 portions.

Ingredients

800g red onion, finely sliced

600g of vine ripened tomatoes, roughly chopped

100g brown sugar

100ml balsamic vinegar

50g salted butter

Method

In a large pan, melt the butter before adding the tomatoes and onion, cooking gently until softened.

Add the brown sugar and balsamic vinegar to the pan and turn up the heat to reduce the mixture.

Once reduced to a sticky syrup, keep stirring as not to burn the chutney in the pan.

Following this step, pour the chutney into a bowl and leave to cool in the fridge for at least 4 hours.

Remove later to serve and enjoy!

Brewed to PERFECTION

Stokes Coffee have years of experience in brewing the finest teas and coffees from exotic locations throughout the world and bringing them to Lincolnshire.

One of Lincolnshire's oldest establishments, Stokes Coffee has been around since 1902 and four generations later, the Stokes family are still giving visitors an authentic taste of Lincolnshire history. Specialising in freshly roasted coffee and selected teas both made in house and imported from around the world; this influential coffee house is also situated inside a one-of-a-kind Tudor building which sits on the medieval High Bridge above the River Witham.

Robert William Stokes has an almost legendary status in the city of Lincoln, founding the company out of his passion and interest in coffee to create what is now an iconic landmark for locals and tourists alike. The history of the quaint half-timbered building and the business itself is well documented as well as continuously celebrated by the Stokes family. Now-retired grandson David Peel and his own sons Adrian and Nick maintain the careful art of expert roasting to make the delicious coffee which Stokes is famed for, allowing the legacy to live on.

Today, the High Bridge café has become an award-winning haunt for Lincolnshire's coffee lovers who can also check in to the Stokes Collection Café which opened in 2011, inside the Collection Museum. Currently under the helm of Nick and manager Jean-Sebastien Braen, Stokes was recently named as the 2014 'Best Tea Room and Coffee Shop' by the Taste Of Excellence awards which was voted for by Lincolnshire's loyal customers. If the rich aroma of fresh ground coffee beans isn't enough to capture your senses, the friendly-family service from the dedicated staff, locally-sourced lunch menu and traditional architecture will certainly do the trick to make you appreciate Lincolnshire's heart... whether you find it at the bottom of a coffee cup or in the pristine views of the river.

Stokes houses their own award-winning loose-leaf Gold Medal tips and speciality teas such as 'Flo's Mix' as well as their own roasted and blended coffee – much of which is exported to many other venues in the Lincolnshire area and cafés around the UK. Stokes exploration has even lead them to discover the coveted fragrant beans from destinations such as Jamaica, Kenya and Nicaragua.

You can warm your cockles with Stokes creamy, smooth Italian inspired cappuccino or latte, sample an exotic imported blend, enjoy a cup-full of joe brewed with their own roasted beans or sip one of their classic English teas; all whilst indulging in their warm, freshly baked scones, local Lincolnshire cheese and plum bread, prepared sandwiches or salads from their kitchen, which are all made with quality Lincolnshire ingredients.

Stokes Coffee
FAMOUS SCONES

What better to accompany a cup of tea or coffee than a good old fashioned English scone. Stokes' legendary Lincolnshire version uses a classic recipe which has been handed down through the generations for a perfect fruit scone. Perfect for slathering in jam and clotted cream, Stokes have this recipe nailed to perfection. Makes 6 to 8 large scones.

Ingredients

100g of butter

300g of self-raising flour

1 pinch of salt

1 egg

100ml whole milk

70g sugar

70g sultanas

Method

Preheat the oven to 200°C and line a baking sheet with baking parchment.

Sift together the flour and salt.

Add the butter and rub it in with your fingertips until the mixture is crumbly.

Mix the sugar and sultanas together before adding to the mixture.

Lightly beat the egg and milk together in a small jug with a fork.

Make a well in the centre of the flour and gradually add the milk and egg mixture with a wooden spoon. Mix until everything comes together and roll out the batter with a rolling pin.

Using a pastry cutter, cut out thick scones from your rolled out pastry making each scone approximately 2 cm thick.

Brush the scones with milk before transferring to the oven and baking for about 12-15 minutes.

Once baked, the scones should be golden brown. Transfer from the oven to a cooling rack and eat on the same day.

Fancy a BREW?

Teaspoon Tea Company are one of Lincolnshire's newest but most sorely welcomed teashops. Opened in March 2014 in Grantham, the shop owned by Pamela and Lance Merryweather is modern in style, with a relaxed environment.

Home to around 40 loose leaf teas ranging from blended black and oolong to green and herbal, Teaspoon Tea Company abandon the usual vintage twee style of many other tea shops for a cool, contemporary setting that puts focus solely on their hand-selected, delicious loose-leaf teas.

A cuppa at Teaspoon allows guests to enjoy the tea exactly how it was meant to be; with the flavours, care and precision which makes perfect cup. Served in clean, white crockery with a tea timer that allows you to brew your tea for just the right amount of time, Teaspoon Tea also have a fully stocked cake counter stocked with Victoria sandwich cakes, chocolate cakes and Grantham ginger cake which are all made in house. They are the perfect accompaniment to a brew, at any time of day.

For the savoury offering, the team at Teaspoon Tea turn tradition on its head by adapting the usually sweet-scone recipe with ingredients such as spinach and artichoke, or ham and tomato, for a unique lunch made by their own fair hands. Cut into wedges and served up with butter, cheese and a choice of chutneys, Teaspoon Tea is the perfect hide-away to relax, embrace and enjoy traditional teas in a whole new way.

Teaspoon consider their high ratings on social media a real achievement when it comes to their success and they have won a number of fans from across the country as well as their native Lincolnshire. The people of Grantham and beyond have taken to Teaspoon Tea with plenty of enthusiasm, leading the company to sell bags of their tea as well as tea pots in store.

There is something distinctly British about enjoying a good cup of tea and when it comes to Teaspoon, they will show you how to enjoy tea like never before.

Teaspoon Tea Company
ARTICHOKE AND SPINACH SAVOURY SCONES

Enjoy traditional British scones with a difference. Tea Spoon Tea Company revolutionise the concept with their savoury ingredients for a unique signature tea-time essential. Makes 6.

Ingredients

75g margarine, chilled and cut into cubes

350g self-raising flour

1 ½ tsp of baking powder

150g of grated cheese

150ml of milk

5 cubes of frozen spinach

¼ of a jar of artichoke in olive oil

Method

Preheat the oven to 200°C.

Place the spinach in a microwavable bowl and cook in the oven for 2 minutes. Drain and leave to cool.

Cut the artichoke into small pieces and set aside.

Sift the flour and the margarine in a bowl and mix until it resembles breadcrumbs; this can be done either by hand or using a mixer.

Add the grated cheese and mix well before adding the cooled spinach and artichoke. Mix this evenly.

Add the milk to the dry now-fully mixed ingredients and stir in, mixing further to form a soft dough ball.

Chaff the dough (gently fold) and knead gently before placing on a baking tray.

Flatten the dough with a depth around 4cm and mould into a round shape.

Place this on a baking tray and bake in the oven for 25 minutes.

Remove from the oven and from the baking tray, allowing the dough to cool completely before slicing into six wedges.

Serve each piece with butter, slices of cheddar cheese and your favourite chutney. We use chutneys from A Little Luxury in Lincolnshire.

Allergy Information:

Contains: gluten, eggs, milk

Into The WOODS

Hailing from a family of farmers, Tom Wood decided his path lay in brewing beer, not selling grain.

Tom Wood's brewery is nestled in the heart of the Lincolnshire Wolds. For 100 years and 3 generations the Woods' family have been farmers by trade at Melton Highwood Farm until youngest Grandson Tom decided his passion was in brewing beer and was inspired to open his own brewery on the land.

Today Tom's brewery produces quality beers and ales using the finest English ingredients infused with a distinctly Lincolnshire spirit and flavour.

Tom's vision was to create something unique and interesting, using the best quality local ingredients to pay homage to his home County of Lincolnshire. Tom's dream was realised when the brewery opened for business in 1995.

The four Woods' brothers chose very different paths in life but each have contributed to the success of the business, which celebrates its 20th anniversary this year. Eldest brother John supplied Tom with malt barley from the farm to kickstart his earliest brewing creations whilst second son, David sold the beers in his pub The Butchers Arms. The beers proved to be a hit with locals and soon the now well-known Lincoln Gold and Bomber County (a nod to Lincolnshire's RAF heritage and also third brother Paul's career as a pilot), were common requests across the bar.

Tom decided to open his own pub in 2003 to showcase the great beers the brewery was creating. The Yarborough Hunt in Brigg is a wonderfully homely and rustic pub. It sells all the rich colourful beers and ales from the brewery as well as products from other local and regional breweries. The cosy setting and welcoming family atmosphere has won them countless awards.

Tom Wood Beers sources all its ingredients as locally as possible. Water for the beer is drilled from a bore hole right on the farm itself and hops are sent from Worcestershire and Kent. No waste is spared as the malt goes to feed the herd of cows that produce Cote Hill Lindum cheese, another Lincolnshire delicacy, that is also rind washed in Tom Wood's ale.

The team make regular appearances at local farmers markets as well as local events such as the Brocklesby Country Fair and the ever-expanding Lincolnshire Show. Tom, his wife Nicky and the rest of the team work with other Lincolnshire businesses to establish a community which honours Lincolnshire as one of the best and biggest counties for great produce.

From their best-selling fresh and hoppy Best Bitter, to the fruity zest of Lincoln Gold, Tom Wood Beers are proponents of good beer using quality local produce, all put together with a whole heap of passion and dedication.

Tom Wood Brewery

Tom Woods' ALE ICE-CREAM

You like ice cream? You like ale? Then what could be better than combining the two. This great recipe is from our friend, chef Colin McGurran of Winteringham Fields, who has always been a great supporter of our brewery. Serves 8.

Ingredients

475ml whipping cream

350ml milk

200g caster sugar

1 vanilla bean and/or 1 tsp vanilla extract

6 egg yolks

330ml Tom Wood ale

Method

Combine the cream, milk, and sugar in a saucepan over medium heat, stirring until the sugar dissolves.

Split the vanilla bean lengthwise with a sharp knife and scrape the tiny black seeds from inside the pod into the cream mixture, also throwing the bean pod into the mix.

Let the mixture come just to a boil before removing from the heat and discarding the spent vanilla pod.

Beat the egg yolks in a heat-proof bowl until thoroughly blended.

Temper the egg yolks by whisking 60ml of hot cream mixture into them;, repeating three more times. In total you should have whisked 240ml of the vanilla cream into the yolks.

Whisk the egg yolk mixture back into the saucepan containing the vanilla cream and place the saucepan over a medium heat.

Keep whisking the mixture constantly until the mixture thickens slightly for about 2-3 minutes. The mixture should coat the back of a spoon when dipped in.

Take care not to let the mixture boil. Transfer the cream mixture into a bowl.

Chill the mixture in the bowl until cold for a minimum of two hours or overnight.

Pour the Tom Wood ale into a saucepan and simmer over low heat for about 15 minutes until reduced to around 160ml. If this does not reach desired amount during this time, simmer for a further five minutes.

Chill the ale syrup for least two hours or overnight.

When the cream and ale syrup are both thoroughly chilled, whisk the ale syrup into the cream mixture.

Pour into an ice cream maker and freeze the mixture according to manufacturer's directions.

When machine has finished churning the ice cream, pack the ice cream into an airtight container and store in the freezer to serve later.

Down on THE FARM

Named after a close family friend, Uncle Henry's has built a reputation for producing and selling wonderful local food.

The name Uncle Henry's evokes images of a familiar warm and welcoming haven with a strong family spirit. For Meryl and Steve Ward, that is exactly how this award-winning Lincolnshire farm shop, butchery and café began life. Managed by their daughter Emma today, Uncle Henry's describes itself as 'the heart of good food' and is all about great-tasting home-produced food which is made with Lincolnshire's wonderful local ingredients, many of which are produced on their family-run farm.

Situated next to the village of Grayingham in north Lincolnshire, Uncle Henry's was aptly named after their family friend Henry Wright who lived in the house behind the existing farm shop and café. His family had lived and farmed the land for 100 years until the Ward family took on the land in 1991, allowing the two families to grow close.

Steve and Meryl's children became very fond of Mr. Wright and would often ask to play at 'Uncle Henry's' house. The name stuck, and they eventually named their blossoming business after him, converting the derelict 19th century limestone building in 2006 into the shop, butchery and café which stand today. Steve and Meryl manage the farm providing much of Uncle Henry's prize winning pork and potatoes. Emma manages the business side of Uncle Henry's to provide great customer service, good value food and fresh produce, making a positive difference in their community.

Uncle Henry's supports over 45 other Lincolnshire producers by stocking their handmade, hand-reared artisan products including beef, lamb, poultry and game which is butchered in store. Their own home-reared Hampshire cross breed of pigs provide the pork for which they are famed.

Their deli ham, haslet and sausage rolls are local favourites whilst their Scotch eggs are award-winning. In 2014, the BBC's One Show awarded them with the title of Best Sausage in The UK and this year they were made finalists for Britain's Best Butcher's Shop whilst Select Lincolnshire named them the 2015/16 Retailer and Producer of The Year. They also work with a number of Lincolnshire chocolatiers, breweries and bakeries to complement their delicious home-produce which has successfully created a mutually sustainable community. Their local bee-keeper Bob Mould even provides the honey sold in their farm shop whilst the cereal crops grown on their land go towards feeding their pigs.

Uncle Henry's are definitely community-minded when it comes to food. Their work in educating the future generation is remarkable, accommodating up to 40 school visits per year around the farm and walled gardens on site, Uncle Henry's is CEVAS accredited, with a 'Learning Outside The Classroom' badge to give the children in the area a unique and enjoyable look into a working farm.

Always efficient and conscious of their carbon-footprint, Uncle Henry's go that extra green mile. Whether it's ensuring the great taste of their products or the friendly atmosphere of the farm, here's one place you can fully rely on for an honest 'farm to fork experience'.

Uncle Henrys
PORK FILLET STUFFED WITH
PEAR AND BLACK PUDDING WITH CIDER SAUCE

This dish is one of Uncle Henry's specialities, served up with sausage meat bon bons, fondant sweet potatoes and Lincolnshire asparagus. Serves 4.

Ingredients

For the pork:

800g Uncle Henry's pork fillet

250g Uncle Henry's black pudding ring, skin removed

250g Uncle Henry's streaky bacon

4 fresh sage leaves, cut into strips

Pinch of salt and freshly ground black pepper

2 tbsp olive oil

4 sweet potatoes, peeled and cut into circles

For the pear and cider sauce:

25g butter

1 tbsp muscovado sugar

3 pears, peeled and quartered with cores removed

1 tbsp olive oil

1 onion, peeled and finely chopped

150g button mushrooms, finely sliced

1 bouquet garni (celery, parsley, bay leaf and thyme tied together with kitchen string)

250ml cider

2 tbsp English mustard

200ml double cream

2 tbsp flat leaf parsley, roughly chopped

For the asparagus:

500g asparagus tips

For the bon bons:

250g Uncle Henry's Lincolnshire sausage meat

2 free-range eggs

8 tbsp panko breadcrumbs

8 tbsp walnuts, chopped

150g Cote Hill Blue cheese

100g flour

Method

Preheat the oven to 180°C.

Slice the pork fillet down the middle lengthways, taking care not to cut all the way through, forming a pocket down its length. Roll the black pudding into a sausage shape and stuff into the pocket of the pork loin. Place a sheet of cling film onto your work surface and lay out the bacon on top, overlapping the slices slightly to form a rectangular sheet of meat. Lay the stuffed loin onto the sheet of bacon, across the end of the rashers. Lay the sage leaves over the top of the pork and season with salt and freshly ground black pepper.

Roll up the fillet to wrap inside the bacon using the cling film to help. Gently roll the wrapped pork loin onto an oiled baking sheet, tucking the ends of the bacon underneath the roll and removing the cling film in the process. Heat the oil in a frying pan and place the pork loin roll into the pan. Sear the pork for 3-4 minutes all over and then cook in the oven for 20-25 minutes, or until cooked through. Once cooked, remove the pork from the oven and set aside to rest for at least 10 minutes.

To begin the pear and cider sauce, melt the butter in a frying pan over a medium heat until it begins to foam, then add the sugar and cook for 1-2 minutes until the sugar is melted, forming a golden brown caramel. Add the pears to the pan and cook for about 10 minutes until tender, turning the pears over occasionally to coat in the caramel. Remove the pan from the heat and set aside.

Heat another frying pan, add the olive oil and fry the onions for 3-4 minutes until softened. Add the mushrooms and cook for a further 1-2 minutes until softened. Add the bouquet garni, cider and mustard; seasoning with salt and freshly ground black pepper. Bring to the boil, before reducing to a simmer and cook for a further 10-12 minutes, or until the liquid has reduced by half. Stir in the cream, flat leaf parsley and any cooking juices from the pork. Add the caramelised pears and heat through. Keep warm.

To begin making the fondant sweet potatoes, cut the sweet potatoes into 2cm thick rounds. Using a circular cutter, cut out discs from the rounds and cut off the sharp edges to create barrel shapes. Melt the butter in a hot pan until foaming, adding the garlic and thyme. Fry for 1 minute, then add the sweet potato rounds and cook for a further 2-3 minutes until browned on one side. Flip the rounds over and carefully add the stock to the pan. Season with salt and freshly ground black pepper, simmering for 10-15 minutes until tender.

For the bon bons, roll the sausage meat into small balls and flatten into a patty shape around 3cm in diameter. Place a small piece of Cote Hill Blue cheese in the centre of the patty and then mould the sausage meat around, rolling to reform a ball. Dip the sausage meat balls into flour, then egg, followed by a mixture of breadcrumbs and walnut pieces. Deep fry in vegetable oil for 2-3 minutes.

Meanwhile, blanche the asparagus tips in a pan of boiling salted water for 3-4 minutes until tender. To serve, cut the pork loin into conical wedges and place two pieces on the plate to cross each other, adding the asparagus into the groove created before placing the fondant potatoes and bon bon's around. Drizzle with the cider sauce and serve immediately.

Lincolnshire's FINEST

Celebrating the taste of Lincolnshire is a passion for the Village Limits country pub, sourcing their food from the surrounding area is more than just good business sense.

A quaint country pub, restaurant and hotel, Village Limits has almost everything you need to get a true taste of Lincolnshire. Whether it be a dish from their locally-sourced menu or a friendly, Lincolnshire welcome as you check in to the rustic, country inn; Village Limits are the proud four-time winners of the Lincolnshire Food & Drink 'Best Pub' Award with countless online reviews testifying to their hospitality.

Located in Woodhall Spa, Billy and Sonia Gemmell took ownership of the pub back in 2006 and have since transformed it into a peaceful family-run business which reflects their passion for promoting Lincolnshire's unique and varied produce.

For Billy, the growth of Village Limits has been especially personal as he began working as a washing up boy at the age of 14 in the very kitchen in which he now oversees. Today, he pieces together a sustainable and rich menu filled with locally-sourced meats, seasonal vegetables and fish from Grimsby docks. The idea was to reduce the carbon footprint of their menu by importing most of their seasonal ingredients from within a 30-mile radius. This includes everything from the meat used in their best-selling steak and ale pies to the potatoes used for their twice-cooked chips and their ice-cream supplied by award-winning creamery Dennetts.

When the team at Village Limits aren't busy scooping 'Best Period Menu' at the annual 1940s Weekend for their simple and original old-fashioned recipes, they're receiving Silver Awards for their cosy accommodation and sharing their local knowledge of the lush country surroundings with guests. Billy has always felt that it was important to support local businesses and Village Limits works consistently hard to keep Lincolnshire traditions alive in both their food and friendliness. As both Billy and his wife grew up in nearby villages, their love for Lincolnshire and its classic dishes runs strongly through everything they turn a hand to.

Village Limits

RABBIT AND JUNIPER BERRY TERRINE, WITH A HANDPICKED FIG AND PEAR COMPOTE

Using two of Lincolnshire's most traditional and distinctive flavours, rabbit and juniper, this contemporary terrine is a unique dish perfect for a dinner party. Created using hand-picked local ingredients, this dish is sure to impress.

Ingredients

2 whole rabbits, roughly chopped with loins removed – keep the bones for stock

10g finely ground juniper berries

300g streaky bacon

For the stock:

2 sticks celery, roughly chopped

1 leek, roughly chopped

2 carrots, roughly chopped

1 onion, roughly chopped

2 tbsp fresh thyme

To marinade the rabbit:

Pomace oil

1 tbsp crushed garlic

For the compote:

6 fresh figs, diced

2 fresh pears, peeled, cored and diced

250ml cooking Port

100ml apple juice

75g caster sugar

¼ tsp ground ginger

Method

For the terrine:

Place the meat into a shallow tray and cover with pomace oil. Add the garlic and seasoning to taste. Cover with cling film and allow meat to marinate in the fridge for up to 24 hours.

Place a large pan on a high heat to brown the bones.

Add in the vegetables and one tablespoon of thyme before covering with 2 pints of water.

Bring to the boil, then turn down the heat to simmer for 2½ hours, until liquid has reduced by half. Use a fine sieve to strain off the liquid and place the liquid in the fridge to cool.

When the rabbit has marinated, thoroughly drain off the oil and place all the meat except the loins into a bowl.

Add in the crushed juniper berries and the rest of the freshly chopped thyme.

Oil a terrine mould or loaf tin, then cover with a layer of cling film ensuring there are no gaps and that there is enough cling film on either side to fold over the top of the terrine.

Next line the mould with the streaky bacon, again ensuring no gaps and enough to cover the top of the terrine.

Fill the terrine halfway up with the rabbit meat mixture, then place the loins lengthways across the mixture, repeating the process with the remaining meat.

Steadily pour in the stock until it just covers the mixture.

Fold the envelope of bacon over the top so that there are no gaps to create an even finish.

Repeat this step with the cling film, then place the terrine lid on top.

Wrap the terrine with a double layer of tin foil, and place into a deep baking tray.

Fill the tray with water until it covers two thirds of the way up the side of the terrine.

Place into a preheated oven at 160°C for 1½-2 hours, or until cooked.

For the compote:

In a medium pan, combine all the compote ingredients over a high heat.

When the liquid starts to boil, reduce to a low heat and stir often but gently for 30 minutes or until the figs have started to break down.

Decant the compote into a suitable container and refrigerate until chilled.

Bread for EXCELLENCE

Well known and well loved by locals, Welbourne's Bakery has over three generations of baking experience.

Welbourne's Bakery is one of the oldest standing bakeries in the county of Lincolnshire and after three generations they still consider themselves a traditional corner shop bakery. Peter Welbourne began working in the bakery in the 1960s, running the shop with his wife Mary for many years. Armed with the original bread recipe used by Peter's grandfather, father, and uncle for decades; a recipe which is still a huge part of the business today.

On Pete's retirement , Welbourne's was bought by a local business, The Elite Fish and Chip Company owned by Adrian Tweedale and his family. Adrian appreciated the roots of the bakery and has sought to keep the nostalgia of the business and his own influence working together perfectly. Collectively they all share the heart and soul of this well-loved traditional bakery, bringing an even brighter future to Welbourne's and their reputation continues to flourish.

Even after retirement Pete still loves baking bread and gets a real kick out of demonstrating his family recipes for charity, local schools and food shows. It is clear that the passion for his work is still as strong as ever and that the bakery, which has stood for over one hundred years, is likely to stand for one hundred more.

Steeped in tradition with many of today's products being created from original recipes by Cornelius Welbourne, who began the business back in 1896. Even now the Welbourne approach to loyal service as well as their quality home-made bread remains largely unchanged.

Jack would mix 20 stone of dough each day by hand to be used for their fresh loaves. This was no easy task in the pre-war days when Welbourne's functioned without a mixer. This meant that even in his 80s, Jack Welbourne had 'forearms like Popeye' from hand-kneading and preparing their signature bread before it was baked in their traditional coal ovens.

The introduction of electric ovens has allowed them to start creating different types of loaves using seeds, toppings and shapes for a more varied selection. A thriving wholesale business sees them deliver their special plum bread, freshly baked loaves and cakes all over the county as well as in Cambridgeshire and Nottinghamshire.

Peter also began making use of the local produce to craft meat pies using distinctive Lincolnshire flavours such as rabbit and red currant, steak and game for a truly delicious, freshly baked experience.

However, one thing that Welbourne's is famed for is their award-winning distinctive 'special plum bread' which has travelled the world over, introducing this uniquely delicious Lincolnshire dish to generation after generation. In fact, both Henry Kissinger and Dickie Bird breakfasted on Welbourne's Bakery products in the 1980s and sampled Welbourne's plum bread which resulted in them giving the recipe a celebrity seal of approval.

Welbourne's special plum bread is dated for 100 days and can be kept for much longer, becoming more and more delicious as it matures. It was only used to be a treat for Christmas and Easter but became so popular due to its rich and extraordinary flavour, that it is now made all year round and has been posted abroad by customers to their loved ones.

Their philosophy is simple yet successful; produce the highest quality products using top class ingredients and give the very best personal service.

LARGE
WHITE DUSTY
£1.65

SMALL
WHITE FARMHOUSE
£1.00

CHICKEN &
MUSHROOM SLICE
£1.45

CHEESE &
ONION ROLL
£1.00

Welbourne Bakery
TRADITIONAL WHITE CRUSTY LOAF

Discover what freshly baked, homemade bread really tastes like with this classic crusty loaf which is the same recipe Welbourne's has baked with since 1896. Simple and satisfying, this delicious loaf is the perfect accompaniment to a soup or stew. For two large or four small loaves.

Ingredients

1.5kg strong white bread flour
28g vegetable fat
28g fresh yeast
825ml warm water
Fat (olive oil, vegetable oil, white shortening, lard or butter)
Pinch of Salt

Method

Place the flour, salt, fat and yeast into a large bowl and mix, breaking up the fat and yeast.

Add three quarters of the water and mix using your finger tips.

Slowly add the rest of the water until the mixture reaches a stiff, chewing-gum like consistency. Note that some flours use a little more or less water

Knead, stretch and pull the dough for 10 minutes. You can use an electric mixer with a dough hook if you prefer.

If you wish to experiment with different flavours or additional ingredients, add them at this point before proceeding to the next step.

Cover with a clean cloth and stand in a warm place for 30-40 minutes to prove until the dough has doubled in size.

Tip your dough out onto a floured surface and press as much air out of the dough as you can.

Shape into loaves of your choice. This process provides you with a traditional crusty loaf which you can mark and sprinkle with flour or leave plain.

For any desired toppings you wish to use, brush the top of your loaves with egg or water before adding the toppings.

After you have shaped your loaf, let it stand again in a warm place for about 30 minutes until it doubles in size once more. Preheat the oven to 230°C (220°C fan).

Bake your loaf for approximately 30 minutes. This may vary depending on the size.

To test the loaf is baked, tap the bottom with your knuckle to check that it makes a hollow sound.

Have a FIELDS DAY

"Have I gone mad?"
"I'm afraid so, but let me tell you something, the best people usually are."
– Lewis Carroll, Alice in Wonderland

When Colin and Bex McGurran took over Winteringham Fields in a sleepy village just north of Scunthorpe, most thought they had gone mad. Coming not long after an almost disastrous venture at the 45-bedroomed Stoneleigh Hotel in Wakefield, the task of putting their own stamp on someone else's life's work may have appeared, to some, a somewhat impulsive pursuit.

But there was something different about Winteringham. With acres of land on their doorstep, a close-knit community feel and charm in abundance, the McGurrans knew they had found home. It was already a firmly established business; with chef Germain Schwab and his wife Annie at the helm of the successful Michelin two-starred restaurant, Colin and Bex were not about to let that legacy trail off when the business was handed over.

At first keeping the model virtually the same, it was only when the recession of 2008 hit that they decided things needed to be shaken up. Modernising the Victorian décor, yet not sacrificing the Alice in Wonderland feel that suited the nooks and crannies of the building, the McGurrans decided to run with the 'down the rabbit hole' theme. Yorkshire artist Tina Antcliffe was employed to add the Lewis Carroll style illustrations and quotes that adorn the walls, injecting a sense of fun and adventure into proceedings.

But the biggest change came when implementing Colin's 'field to fork' philosophy. Armed with the knowledge that local produce is infinitely better for the environment, bursting with flavour and economically sensible, Colin was struck with the notion of producing his own food after realising every morsel on his English breakfast one morning could be sourced right there in the village.

Fast forward to today, and you'll find a restaurant that is virtually self-sufficient from its own fully working farm and gardens, with staff dividing their time between the kitchen and the fields – and enjoying every minute. "Working in the fields and with the animals has taken us all so much closer to nature," Colin explains, "and we have a true affinity with whatever we are preparing for the table."

And this is why the food served at Winteringham is exceptional. Motivated, passionate and determined to get the best out of seasonal ingredients in the most creative way possible, the chefs here devise and revise their menus frequently and precisely. The result? Fresh, seasonal and innovative dishes that are deliciously unique to Winteringham and its surroundings.

Winteringham Fields
BUTTERNUT SQUASH VELOUTE

with chestnut cream

Ingredients

For the butternut velouté:

500g butternut squash

50g unsalted butter

Salt

1g truffle oil

For the chestnut cream:

200g double cream

60g cooked chestnuts

2g salt

For the pumpkin seeds:

200g dried pumpkin seeds

50g sugar

For the butternut pieces:

Butternut pieces

Salt and pepper, to season

Butter

Oil

Method

For the butternut velouté

Peel the butternut squash and slice thinly.

Put all ingredients in a pan and cling film to steam until soft.

Blitz in a blender for 2 minutes then pass through a chinois.

To make the chestnut cream

Whisk the cream until softly whipped.

Grate in the cooked chestnuts on a micro plane so very finely grated with the salt.

Continue to whisk until the mixture firms up and everything is fully combined, making sure you don't over whisk.

For the pumpkin seeds

Toast the pumpkin seeds in a pan.

Remove the seeds, add the sugar and then slowly melt in the pan.

As the sugar starts to caramelise, add the pumpkin seeds back in until they are all nicely covered.

Lay out across parchment paper to cool down, and then split up.

For the grilled butternut pieces.

Peel the butternut squash and slice to 1cm thick, square off each piece and cut 1cm strips one way, then 1cm the other way.

Season the pieces and cook on a plancher grill with oil until they start to char.

Add a pinch of butter then turn over and repeat on the other side until nicely cooked.

To serve

Pour the veloute into bowls, add the chestnut cream and scatter the toasted pumpkin seeds and grilled butternut squash pieces on top.

The DIRECTORY

These great businesses have supported the making of this book;
please support and enjoy them.

Bunty's Tea Room
18 Steep Hill
Lincoln, Lincolnshire LN2 1LT
Telephone: 01522 537909
www.buntyslincoln.com
A family-run vintage tea room on Lincoln's Steep Hill which serves delicious home-made cakes and scones.

Doddington Hall
Doddington, Lincolnshire LN6 4RU
Telephone: 01522 694308
www.doddingtonhall.com
Award-winning restaurant, café and farm shop set in the stunning grounds of the Doddington Hall country estate and gardens.

Elite Fish and Chips
2 Grantham Rd, Sleaford NG34 7NB
Telephone: 01529 414534
The Moorland Centre, Tritton Road,
Lincoln LN6 7JW
Tel: 01522 509 505
High Street, Ruskington NG34 9DY
Tel: 01526 832 332
www.elitefishandchips.com
Traditional family run fish and chip shop serving fresh locally and ethically sourced fish.

Fred and Bex
Bolle Cottage, Hoffleet, Stow,
Bicker, Boston, Lincolnshire PE20 3AJ
Telephone: 07917 237127
www.fredandbex.com
A family business which creates, sells and distributes traditional raspberry and blackberry vinegars using home-grown produce.

Harrisons Restaurant
12 Market Place, Barton-Upon-Humber,
North Lincolnshire DN18 5DA
Telephone: 01652 637412
www.harrisons-barton.co.uk
A welcoming family restaurant serving food crafted with Lincolnshire's finest products including vegetables, meat and fish from the county.

The Inn On The Green
34 The Green, Ingham, Lincoln
LN1 2XT
Telephone: 01522 730354
www.innonthegreeningham.co.uk
A fine quality dining experience located in a beautiful historic building in the Lincolnshire Wolds.

Jews House Restaurant
15 The Strait, Lincoln LN2 1JD
Telephone: 01522 524851
www.jewshouserestaurant.co.uk
A luxury restaurant situated in one of Lincolnshire's most iconic buildings.

Lincolnshire Showground
Grange-de-Lings, Lincoln LN2 2NA
Telephone 01522 585513
www.lincolnshireshowground.co.uk
Celebrating the best of the farming and food community in Lincolnshire as well as the home of the well-established Lincolnshire Agricultural Society.

The Livesy Arms
Ludborough, Grimsby,
North East Lincolnshire DN36 5SF
Telephone: 01472 840038
www.theliveseyarms.com
A charming dining destination ran by creative culinary expert Rosie Dicker and her dedicated team.

Mario's
30 S Gate, Sleaford NG34 7RY
Telephone: 01529304430
www.mariospizzagrillsleaford.co.uk
Homely Italian specialising in dishes from the south-east of Italy and the flavours of the Med.

Meridian Meats
108 Eastgate, Louth LN11 9AA
Telephone: 01507 603357
www.meridianmeatsshop.co.uk
The BBC's 2009 Butcher of The Year and award-winning butcher shop in the heart of Louth.

The Original Cake Company
The Bakery, Pioneer Business Park,
Pioneer Way, Lincoln LN6 3DH
Telephone: 01522 69 44 11
www.originalcake.co.uk
Delicious handmade traditional cakes baked with over 150 years of experience.

Petwood Hotel Limited
Stixwould Road, Woodhall Spa,
Lincolnshire LN10 6QG
Telephone: 01526 351900
Website: www.petwood.co.uk
Beautiful turn of the century hotel with a fascinating wartime history, vibrant surrounding gardens and an award-winning restaurant.

Redhill Farm
Laughton Lane, Morton,
Gainsborough, Lincs DN21 3DT
Telephone: 01427 628270
www.redhillfarm.com
Family run farm and shop specialising in ethical, hand-reared free-range pork used in traditional Lincolnshire pork products.

R J Hirst High Class Family Butchers
Station Road, Woodhall Spa,
Lincs LN10 6QL
Telephone: 01526 352321
www.rjhirstfamilybutchers.co.uk
Artisan family-ran butcher shop and farm handmaking and supplying its own classic Lincolnshire sausages.

San Pietro Restaurant with Rooms
11 High Street East,
Scunthorpe, North Lincs DN15 6UH
Telephone: 01724 277 774
www.sanpietro.uk.com
San Pietro combine the finest ingredients of Mediterranean cooking with welcoming family feel.

The Stag Inn
Church St, Barkston NG32 2NB
Telephone: 01400 250363
www.thestagbarkston.co.uk
A cosy and classic old English pub with a roaring fire, wooden beams and traditional British dishes with a twist.

Stokes Tea and Coffee
Mint Lane, Lincoln LN1 1UD
Telephone: 01522 523548
207 High Street, Lincoln LN5 7AU
Tel: 01522 523 548
Danes Terrace, Lincoln LN2 1LP
Tel: 01522 523 548
Website: www.stokes-coffee.co.uk
Dating back to 1902, Stokes Coffee is still providing fresh roasted coffee in one of the city's most distinctive historic buildings.

Teaspoon Tea Company
Unit 8, The George Shopping Centre,
Grantham, Lincolnshire NG31 6LH
Telephone: 07443 537122
www.teaspoon-tea.co.uk
A contemporary tea shop with over 40 specialist loose-leaf teas as well as homemade cakes and scones.

Tom Wood Brewery
Melton High Wood, Barnetby,
North Lincolnshire DN38 6AA
Telephone: 01652 680001
www.tom-wood.com
Carefully crafted specialist ales and beers using Lincolnshire sourced ingredients.

Uncle Henry's
Grayingham Grange Farm,
Grayingham, Gainsborough, Lincs
DN21 4JD
Telephone: 01652640308
www.unclehenrys.co.uk
A warm, welcoming family restaurant with ingredients produced on their own working farm.

Village Limits
Stixwould Road, Woodhall Spa,
Lincolnshire LN10 6UJ
Telephone: 01526 353312
www.villagelimits.co.uk
A quaint and award-winning restaurant, pub and hotel in Woodhall Spa with fantastic countryside views

Welbourne's Bakery
38 High Street, Navenby LN5 0DZ
Telephone: 01522 810239
A family-established and run bakery which is famous for its fresh baked bread which still used the original recipe passed down through three generations.

Winteringham Fields
1 Silver St, Winteringham, North
Lincolnshire DN15 9ND
Telephone: 01724 733096
Run by Great British Menu star Colin McGurran, Winteringham Field's seasonal taster menu is renowned across the UK.

me:ze
PUBLISHING

Other titles in this series

The Sheffield Cook Book features
Baldwin's Omega, Nonna's, Ashoka,
Cubana, Peppercorn.
978-0-9928981-0-6

The Nottingham Cook Book features
Sat Bains with Rooms, World Service,
Harts, Escabeche
978-0-9928981-5-1

The Derbyshire Cook Book features
Chatsworth Estate, Fischers of
Baslow, Thornbridge Brewery
978-0-9928981-7-5

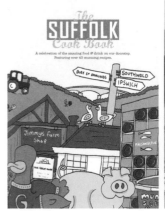

The Suffolk Cook Book featuring
Jimmys Farm, Gressingham Duck etc.
978-1-910863-02-2

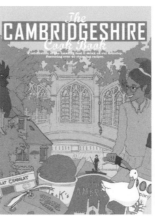

The Cambridgeshire Cook Book
features Midsummer House, The Pint
Shop, Gog Magog Hills, Clare College
978-0-9928981-9-9

The Manchester Cook Book
featuring Aiden Byrne, Simon Rogan,
Masterchef Winner Simon Wood
& lots more. 978-1-910863-01-5

All available from Waterstones, Amazon, independent bookshops
and all establishments featured in the book.

FIND OUT MORE ABOUT MEZE PUBLISHING AT WWW.MEZEPUBLISHING.CO.UK